Instructor's Manual

Mosaic 2

Writing

4th Edition

Prepared by

Diana Renn

McGraw-Hill
Contemporary

McGraw-Hill/Contemporary

*A Division of The **McGraw-Hill** Companies*

Mosaic 2 Writing Instructor's Manual, 4th Edition

Published by McGraw-Hill/Contemporary, a business unit of The McGraw-Hill Companies, Inc., 1221 Avenue of the Americas, New York, NY 10020. Copyright © 2002, 1996, 1990, 1985 by The McGraw-Hill Companies, Inc. All rights reserved. No part of this publication may be reproduced or distributed in any form or by any means, or stored in a database or retrieval system, without the prior written consent of The McGraw-Hill Companies, Inc., including, but not limited to, in any network or other electronic storage or transmission, or broadcast for distance learning.

 This book is printed on recycled, acid-free paper containing 10% postconsumer waste.

1 2 3 4 5 6 7 8 9 0 QPD/QPD 0 9 8 7 6 5 4 3 2 1

ISBN 0-07-248148-X

Editorial director: *Tina B. Carver*

Series editor: *Annie Sullivan*

Development editors: *Nancy Jordan, Annie Sullivan*

Director of marketing: *Thomas P. Dare*

Production and composition: *A Good Thing, Inc.*

Printer: *Phoenix Color*

www.mhcontemporary.com/interactionsmosaic

TABLE OF CONTENTS

Introduction

This book is part of the writing strand of McGraw-Hill/Contemporary's **Interactions Mosaic** series. It is intended for students of English at the advanced level. Students at this level are presumed to have some experience creating simple essays of one or more paragraphs. **Mosaic 2 Writing** will review the elements of paragraph writing and use this as a departure point for writing articles, narratives, and essays of multiple paragraphs.

Mosaic 2 Writing is divided into twelve chapters. The material in each chapter is topically organized. The topics, such as health care, relationships, occupations, and lifestyles, are of relevance and interest to adult learners of English. Each chapter is composed of four parts.

Part 1 Ideas for Writing—The activities in this section are designed to activate schemata and to help students generate ideas for the piece of writing which they will complete by the end of the chapter. The opening page shows a photo or other illustration which you can use as the basis for a discussion on a topic related to the chapter. This will prepare students for the brainstorming and freewriting activities which follow.

Part 2 Language for Writing—This section provides expressions, phrases, and vocabulary which students will find useful in completing the writing activity. Explanatory text is followed by exercises and activities to provide practice in using the targeted forms.

Part 3 Systems for Writing—In this section, students will learn how paragraphs are organized into essays, and how different kinds of writing exhibit different kinds of organization. Students will practice identifying these elements by editing sample essays and other kinds of activities. At the end of this section, students are given a prompt or topic to write about. The following will section will help them to finalize their writing.

Part 4 Evaluating for Writing—These activities provide a context for students to evaluate their own work and the word of a partner. Pairs of students exchange work and use the questions in this section to give each other feedback. These peer conferences provide a good starting point for revisions. Other activities in this section guide students through various aspects of the editorial process when they are ready to begin their rewrites.

General Teaching Suggestions

Mosaic 2 Writing provides students with a wide variety of tips and strategies for clear, effective writing. You can help them assimilate the information in this book by using good teaching practices. Here are a few techniques and strategies you can use with virtually any activity:

- Use volunteers as models and then call on others in the class.
- List important information and words on the board.
- Maintain a lively pace in the class.
- Try to give everyone a chance to participate.

As you review the responses to the activities in the student book, ask volunteers to explain their answers and to justify their responses. If appropriate, have the class look back at the text to verify information and details. In exercises where more than one answer is possible, invite several students to share their responses and ideas.

Groupwork

Small groups allow students more of a chance to participate in discussion activities. It is often easier to speak in a small group than in front of the whole class, so the small group situation is more secure for those who are less proficient in their speaking skills. In addition, it allows time for students to help each other with vocabulary. Students can think and practice saying something in a small group before addressing a larger audience. Groupwork promotes discussion and sharing of ideas and cultural understanding. Students can learn from each other. Groupwork also allows you to address individual needs of students. When students are working in groups, be sure that:

- students understand the directions of the activity

- everyone in the group is involved or has a role
- students show respect for each other
- there is a time limit for the activity
- groups have a chance to share what they discussed or prepared

Divide the class into groups of 4–6 for discussions and group writing activities. Prepare for groupwork. Have the following roles clearly defined for each member of the group:

- *reader,* or *facilitator,* who reads instructions, guides the group, is the leader
- *recorder,* who takes notes on discussions and answers for the activity
- *checker,* who makes sure everyone in the group understands points and watches the time, etc.
- *reporter,* who will share the group's information with the rest of the class.

As groups are working, go around the room listening. You may need to assist with vocabulary or give other guidance. Your job is to facilitate the group activity, not to lead it. Make a note of types of problems that arise and address them later.

Multi-level Classes

Students have different needs and learning styles, so there will usually be a range of levels within a class. By varying the types of activities, you can address the needs of all students. Use whole-class activities for presenting and modeling activities. Allow students to work individually, in pairs, or small groups to practice and prepare responses. During this time, give individual attention as needed. Have students work together in cooperative groups, not competitive groups. In this way, all students will participate, contribute, help, and learn from each other rather than competing against each other. If some students finish classwork activities before others in the class, encourage them to work on the expansion and extension suggestions found at the end of many of the student book exercises. You may want to provide additional reading materials for these advanced learners to browse through if they finish earlier than others. If possible, allow students to explore the Internet for related readings and information to share with the class related to the chapter topics.

You may want to ask students to evaluate their own progress halfway through the course. Ask them to write down if they feel they are making progress and what they feel they have learned so far in the course. Also ask them to write down what they hope to achieve in the second half of the course and how you can best help them achieve their goals. As you read through their self-evaluations, make notes about common goals they have to incorporate into the course. Give students feedback on their progress, too.

Using the Video

The video component provides additional activities related to the chapter topics. Each segment presents some culturally significant concept, fact, or issue. You may choose to use the video at the end of the chapter, as a culminating activity that reinforces listening, speaking, reading, and writing skills. The video section may be used at the beginning of a chapter to present the basic content area and initiate discussion of the basic content. Alternatively, you might find it more appropriate to use the video section to break up the heavy reading content and reading skills exercises in the chapter.

For each video segment there are several activities. The first exercise prepares students for watching the video. Students list vocabulary or share information that they know about the topic. They can make predications about what they will see based on the title and the activity questions. The next two activities guide students as they watch the video at least two times. Students should read the questions before watching so they will know what information they need to find. The video segments are relatively short, so students are encouraged to watch the videos several times. The final video exercise invites students to write on subjects related to the video subject. The tasks become longer and more complex as the students' writing proficiency increases.

Administering the Writing Placement Test

The Writing Placement Test helps teachers and administrators place students into the Writing strand of the **Interactions Mosaic** series. All of the placement tests have been carefully designed to assess a student's language proficiency as it correlates to the different levels of the **Interactions Mosaic** series.

The writing test has been created to assess knowledge about writing, correct usage, and organization. The first three parts consist of multiple-choice tests. Part 1 focuses on knowledge about writing; Part 2, usage; and Part 3, organization.

Part 4 offers suggested topics for writing samples as well as a rubric for assessing the writing samples. There are suggested topics for students to write either a paragraph or an essay depending upon their probable level of proficiency as well as the amount of time allowed for students to do a writing sample. Students at lower levels of proficiency should be given the paragraph topics and at the higher levels the essay topics.

Listed below are suggested levels of placement based only on the multiple-choice test.

The writing samples are assessed more holistically. Use the rubrics and your own judgment to assess where students should be placed based on their writing samples.

Placement Chart for the Writing Test

Number of Items Correct	Place in
0–3	Needs a more basic text.
4–6	Interactions Access
7–12	Interactions 1
13–19	Interactions 2
20–27	Mosaic 1
28–35	Mosaic 2

Using the Chapter Quizzes

The **Mosaic 2 Writing** quizzes allow teachers to assess whether the students have mastered the vocabulary and basic comprehension of the reading passages in the chapters. They also assess how well students can use the real-life reading skills or recognize word categories. In addition, they help asses how well students can use the language to communicate in writing their own ideas and thoughts about the chapter topics.

The **Mosaic 2 Writing** quizzes do not test students' reading comprehension or summarizing skills. The teacher should be assessing and evaluating students' reading skills as they complete the exercises in the chapters.

The quizzes also bring closure to chapters and give students a feeling of achievement and progress as they go through the textbook and course.

Description

There are 12 quizzes, one for each chapter in the reading text. Each quiz contains five sections:

- vocabulary
- ordering sentences
- usage
- reading comprehension
- grammar/mechanics

The first section checks students' understanding of key vocabulary about the chapter topics. The vocabulary items are selected from the reading selections of the chapter. Students match the words with their meanings or synonyms.

In the second section, students are asked to put a group of sentences in a logical order. This is a good way to check students' ability to recognize topic sentences and to organize a simple paragraph.

The third section asks students to discriminate between well-formed and ill-formed sentences. These sentences embody sentence patterns and grammar points addressed throughout the chapter in the student book. The purpose of this section is to test students' knowledge of correct English usage.

The fourth section of the quizzes presents a small reading text which may be created for the quiz or, in some cases, it may be adapted from a passage in the corresponding chapter in the student book. Students are then presented with questions and multiple choice answers about the content of the passage. The questions focus on students' ability to identify the main idea of the passage, the intent of the author or intent of the passage, and the genre or type of writing. Some questions test students' literal comprehension of the text, and others assess critical thinking skills. Students need to be able to recognize and use the words and expressions that are in reading materials around them daily and they need to apply other higher level reading skills.

A major grammar or language structure for each chapter is highlighted in the last section of the quizzes. Students choose the correct word to complete a cloze sentence. Targeted concepts include parts of speech, grammar, punctuation, and writing conventions. Although there are no activities in the student book on these specific points, students need to use them throughout the chapter exercises. The point of this section to help you assess students' knowledge of language about language.

Administration

The quizzes can be duplicated and given to students individually or for full-class administration.

Scoring and Grading

Each section of the quiz is worth 5 points. The total possible score is 25 points.

Language and Learning

Goals

- **Write about an aspect of language learning**
- **Recognize cultural humor**
- **Understand the form and function of an academic essay**
- **Edit for the main idea**
- **Edit for correct essay form and function**

Part 1 Ideas for Writing

Getting Started

1 Page 2.

Have students look at the pictures and discuss them in groups or pairs. Have them first describe where each picture was taken and what the people are doing. Then have them discuss the questions.

2 Page 3.

Have students interview a classmate and take notes. Encourage them to add one or two questions of their own. This activity will be expanded in Part 1 Activity 6, which asks them to interview three people. You can use Activity 2 as a "getting to know you" exercise and then have them expand it later by interviewing two more people. Students can write the results of Activity 2 in a short, informal paragraph and share it with the class, or speak from their notes as a way to introduce their partner to the class.

Reading for Ideas

3 Prereading Questions. Page 5.

Have students write their answers to the prereading questions and share them with a partner or group. Answers will vary. Then have them read the article. You can have them read silently while you read aloud, or you can have them take turns reading each paragraph aloud.

4 Postreading Questions. Page 7.

Have students complete the chart individually, in pairs, or in groups. Encourage them to add examples from their own experience in addition to examples from the article.

Sample Answers:

Factors	Examples
Be aware of your MOTIVE in learning a new language.	If real proficiency is your goal, rather than basic travel phrases, a university or language institute may be the best place to learn.
Consider the METHODS available and decide which one is best for you. Consider the TEACHER	Total immersion may simulate the experience of being in another country.
	Class size usually affects the language learning experience; small classes are often preferred but may not necessarily be the best.
	Private tutoring may work for serious students who lack time.
	Group classes may work well for others who prefer interactive activities.
	A teacher who is a native speaker has advantages, but may not be enthusiastic about teaching.
	A nonnative teacher may understand students' questions better because she has studied the language too and has been in their position.
	Teachers have different levels of training or, in some cases, none at all; you should take time to check credentials.

Answers to questions 1 and 2 will vary; encourage students to write their answers individually and then share them with a group or the class.

Thinking Critically

Have students read the information on **recognizing cultural humor** in the box on page 8 and then discuss their interpretation of the title of the article in groups. See if they can think of other titles for the article that would reflect humorous word play from their own culture. Encourage them to find and share other examples of North American humor. Consider having them keep a log (or keep a class log) of cultural humor, puns, idioms, and proverbs throughout the duration of the course.

Freewriting

5 Page 8.

The concept of freewriting may be new for some students. Tell them that the purpose of freewriting is to generate ideas on the page, and that they should not worry about grammar, spelling, accuracy, or even complete sentences. The purpose is to just keep writing. You might want students to do this type of activity in a separate journal throughout the course. They can turn in journals to you periodically. You can comment on the content and return them before they hand in an assignment, or later. Depending on how much time you have, they could freewrite at home or in class, but it is probably best to have them freewrite in class for a set period of time at first until they become comfortable with the concept. The writing from this particular activity will be used for Part 2 Activity 6 Student Book page 11.

Gathering Information

6 Page 8.

Students can expand on their information gathered from Activity 2 by interviewing two more people in or outside of the class. Or they could interview three native English speakers who also speak a foreign language. Note that this information can also be recycled in Part 2 Activity 5 Student Book page 11, which asks students to write a paragraph about one of the people they interviewed.

7 Page 8.

Have students share their interview results in groups or as a class. They can write their answers to the questions about the interview process, or use them as the basis for their discussions.

Part 2 Language for Writing

Describing Foreign Language Learning

1 Page 9.

Explain to students that they can use these vocabulary words for their own writing and discussion activities in this chapter, and specifically in the subsequent writing activity (Activity 2, page 10). You might encourage them to keep a vocabulary log for the course in which they keep the vocabulary activities for each chapter, as well as definitions of other new words they encounter in the readings. You might also encourage them to write sentences of their own using these new words. Later activities will ask students to write paragraphs incorporating as many new words as possible.

Answers: 1. Creole 2. a multilinguist 3. a practical program 4. proficiency 5. total immersion 6. a dialogue 7. private tutoring 8. a native speaker 9. a criterion 10. the target language 11. a nonnative speaker

2 Page 10.

Have students share their paragraphs in pairs and check each other's use of the new vocabulary words. Let students make corrections before handing in the paragraphs to you.

3 Page 11.

This activity asks students to consider a fictional case of a successful language learner. Encourage them to think of reasons from the article, their discussions, and their own experiences to explain Sotirios's success. Most students at this level should understand the meaning of *topic sentence*, but you may want to check that they comprehend the term and the function of a topic sentence. Explain, if necessary, that it is usually the first sentence of the paragraph, and that it states the controlling idea of the paragraph. As with the previous activity, students can proofread and edit one the paragraphs in pairs before handing them in to you. Note that this activity can be combined with Activity 4 for a longer assignment (see below).

Sample Paragraph:

Sotirios, a foreign student, came to the U.S. from Greece only one year ago speaking no English, but today he speaks fluent English. What accounts for his extraordinary success? There are several reasons. First, he quickly made American friends. Meeting and socializing with people who did not speak his native language forced him to use the target language more quickly than if he socialized only with Greek-speaking people or if he did not socialize at all. His attempt to meet native speakers immediately shows his motivation. Secondly, he knew that it would be important to learn English if he wanted to achieve his goal of attending graduate school in the U.S. Because he always had this goal in mind, he never stopped trying as hard as he could in and outside of his English classes, even when he got discouraged at times. Finally, he attended a language program that he knew would best fit his criteria and aptitude. He spent a lot of time researching programs when he was in Greece, and he chose a practical program with a total immersion program, small classes, highly-trained teachers who are all native speakers, and the option of private tutoring. For these reasons, Sotirios now enjoys his proficiency in English, and has just learned that he was accepted to an American graduate program.

4 Page 11.

This activity asks students to do the same thing as in Activity 3, but to consider the case of an unsuccessful language learner. For a longer activity, you could have students write the two paragraphs as the body of one essay with an introduction and conclusion, or simply have them hand in both paragraphs at once.

5 Page 11.

Have students select one of their interviewees from the language survey at the beginning of the chapter and incorporate new words and expressions. As with the previous two activities, students could proofread one another's paragraphs before handing them in to you, checking specifically for correct use of vocabulary and expressions.

6 Page 11.

This activity asks students to make their freewriting activity a formal writing piece. Assure them that they may not need to use everything they wrote when they shape their ideas into a paragraph, and that they may wish to change the order of their ideas. Or, if they like the way their freewriting turned out, they may wish to keep the general structure but polish the grammar and add new words/expressions where appropriate.

Part 3 Systems for Writing

Essay Form and Function

First elicit what students already know about paragraphs and essays. Then have them read the information in the boxes on page 11. Point out that this chapter focuses on the academic essay, which can be different from the personal essay in that it is more structured. Be sure that students understand the concept of indentation to signal a new paragraph. You might hand out an example of an essay with correctly indented paragraphs versus an incorrect and have students discuss why the indented version is easier to read.

1 Page 12.

Have students work individually, in pairs, or as a class to label the parts in the essay diagram.

Answers: Paragraph 1: introductory paragraph, Paragraph 2: body paragraph, Paragraph 3: body paragraph, Paragraph 4: body paragraph, Paragraph 5: concluding paragraph

2 Page 13.

Have students read the student essay individually or out loud in pairs, alternating paragraphs. Have them label the paragraph types in the margins, underline the thesis, and circle connecting words and phrases. Then have them answer the questions and share them with the class.

Answers:

Paragraph Types: Paragraph 1–introductory paragraph, Paragraphs 2–3 — body paragraphs, Paragraph 5 = concluding paragraph

Thesis statement: The way in which a realistic person achieves this state of mind is by being objective, critical, and highly rational about his or her dreams.

Connecting words and phrases:

Paragraph 1: Thus, on the other hand, on the contrary

Paragraph 2: instead, For example, such as, However, For this reason, For example, Thus

Paragraph 3: In fact, For example, Instead

Paragraph 4: Indeed, For example, However, Therefore

Paragraph 5: also, Not only that

Answers to questions: 1. The main idea of the essay is that realistic people, unlike dreamers and neurotics, are not obsessive about their dreams; instead, they are objective, critical, and highly rational about them.
2. The writer's purpose is a combination of all of the purposes listed. 3. There are transition words within paragraphs, and between the first and second paragraphs. Students can debate whether or not the essay is easy to understand; if so, they should be encouraged to state what aspects in particular contribute to or distract from the essay's readability.

3 Page 14.

For this expansion of a paragraph into an essay, students could choose from any of the paragraphs they wrote in Part 2. Have them outline their essay first, following the diagram. They should write a thesis statement and all three topic sentences in their outlines. Then have students work in pairs to proofread the essay following the questions on page 13.

Focus on Testing

Editing for Correct Form and Function

Explain to students that this section, in this chapter and throughout the book, will help them prepare for timed essay questions on standardized tests. You might have them practice this by giving them one of the writing assignments below the box as a timed writing test, and have them check their own essay according to the criteria for form and function.

Writing Assignments. Page 15.

Have students choose one of these topics for a writing assignment to complete at home or, alternatively, in class as a timed essay. If you give this as a homework assignment, encourage students to use their freewriting, discussion notes, and paragraph assignments to help them with content for the assignment. Also encourage students to write an outline, thesis statement, and topic sentences before beginning the assignment; you may even wish to have students turn in an outline to you before they do the actual writing. Check to be sure that each paragraph is on a distinctly different topic, or have students check for this in pairs. Note that topics 5 and 6 lend themselves more to personal narration than the first four topics, which are more formal in structure and tone.

Part 4 Evaluating for Rewriting

Be sure that students are all familiar with the vocabulary for describing the writing process: drafting (first, second, and final drafts), editing, proofreading, and revising. If students are unfamiliar with or seem uncomfortable with the concept of peer reviewing a draft, you may wish to devote some class time to going over guidelines for ensuring a positive, constructive atmosphere, as well as reassuring students that helping a peer improve his or her paper will help them to improve their own writing and editing skills. Allow for plenty of class time for this activity. Students will be evaluating each other's drafts with particular criteria in mind for each stage of this process. Students can conduct peer reviews in a variety of ways, in pairs and small groups, orally and in writing; they may choose their own pairs or be assigned a partner by yourself. They could switch partners/groups between drafts, or remain with the same ones. They could read their work aloud or have their partners read silently. You may wish to vary the structure of peer review sessions throughout the course.

Evaluating the First Draft. Page 16.

Have students read the drafts silently and discuss the questions. They may find it useful to take notes on the questions to aid them in discussion.

Evaluating the Second Draft. Page 16.

Step 1 will likely work best if students write their answers, as they are looking for very specific things. Students can show their answers to the author of the paper, or hold a discussion based on their answers.

Writing the Final Draft. Page 18.

Consider having students keep a portfolio of their finished work to be turned in at the end of the course. This way they will have a record of their progress.

Video Activities: The School for Success

Before You Watch

Have students discuss the questions in groups. Encourage them to give specific examples of the way in which school, home life, and parents can contribute to children's academic success. Answers will vary.

Watch [on video]

Play the video. Have students listen for the answers and write them. Play the video again, if necessary. Have students compare their answers in groups.

Answers: 1. The School of Success
2. children and their parents 3. c 4. a, b, d

Watch Again [on video]

Play the video. Have students listen for the answers and write them. Play the video again, if necessary. Have students compare their answers in groups.

Answers: 1. a 2. c 3. b 4. a

After You Watch

You might have students debate the question first in their groups in order to help them generate ideas and opinions for their essays. They could hold a formal debate, with two sides listing reasons for/against the issue, or talk informally, agreeing and disagreeing with one another in a more conversational fashion. Once they have decided on their position, have them state their opinion in one thesis statement. Encourage them to write an outline of supporting reasons, as well as topic sentences for each paragraph, before beginning to write. One way they could organize their ideas is to list their reasons that support their opinion, and then organize the reasons in the order of importance, building up to the most important. You could have students hand in their outlines first, or have partners compare and give feedback on outlines.

Danger and Daring

Goals

- Research and write about an explorer's adventures and motivation
- Plan a thesis statement with a topic and angle
- Edit for the main idea and thesis statement
- Learn how to use prediction as a critical thinking skill

Part 1 Ideas for Writing

Getting Started

1 **Page 22.**
   Have students look at the pictures and read the captions. Have them complete the information chart in pairs or groups, or have them do it individually and compare their answers with others. If students do not find information in the captions about the specific time of the event, have them give an approximate time based on when the person lived.

Answers:

Who Was This Explorer?	Where was S/he From?	Where Did the Person Travel? What Did the Person do?	When Did S/He Do It?
Annie Smith Peck	The United States	She climbed the highest peak in Peru	She did this in 1930 when she was sixty years old.
Delia J. Akeley	The United States	She traveled across Africa and lived with indigenous people.	Sometime during the late 19th century or the early 10th century.
Louise Arner Boyd	The United States (California)	She led several scientific expeditions to Greenland.	Sometime during the early 20th century.
Marco Polo	Italy	He wrote about his travels to Asia and introduced Europe to The Far East.	In the 1200s.
Mary Kingsley	England	She traveled to West Africa.	The end of the 19th century.
Amelia Earhart	The United States (Kansas)	She was the first woman to fly alone across the Atlantic Ocean	1932
Yuri Gargarin	Russia	He was the first person to travel in space.	1961
Neil Armstrong	The United States	He walked on the moon.	1969
Arlene Blum	The United States	She climbed to the top of Nepal's Annapurna 1 with a group of women hikers.	1978
Sir Edmund Hillary	New Zealand	He climbed to the summit of Mount Everest.	1953

Have students answer questions 1–5 and write their answers. Then have them share their answers with a group or a partner.

2 Page 25.
Have students work in groups to think of additional explorers. If time allows, you might have them try to find pictures of/information about the additional explorers to share with the class on the Internet or the library.

Reading for Ideas

3 Prereading Questions. Page 25.
Have students write their answers to the prereading questions and share them with a partner or group. Answers will vary. Then have them read the article. You can have them read silently while you read aloud, or you can have them take turns reading each paragraph aloud as a class or in groups.

4 Postreading Questions. Page 28.
Have students complete the chart individually, in pairs, or in groups. Be sure that they understand the meaning of summarize and skim. To summarize is to give only the main ideas of a text. To skim is to read quickly, sometimes looking for particular kinds of information.

Answers:

Who Was She?	Where was She From?	Where Did She Travel? What Did the She do?	When Did She Do It?
Alexandra David Neel	France	Made numerous journeys across the high Tibetan plateau. She disguised herself as a Tibetan beggar and hiked over 2000 miles to the forbidden city of Lhasa.	She made her journeys from 1911–1944. Her journey to Lhasa was made when she was 55 years old.
Fanny Bullock Workman	The United States (Massachusetts)	She traveled and explored in the Himalayas with her husband, and advanced the suffragist cause.	She journeyed between 1890 and 1915.
Annie S. Peck	The United States	She climbed the Matterhorn and later was the first to climb the Huascaran in the Peruvian Andes; she claimed she set a record for the highest altitude for an American.	She climbed the Matterhorn when she was 45. She climbed the Huascaran in 1908, when she was 58.
Claude Kogan	France	She led the first attempt by a woman's team to climb an 8,000-meter peak. She and three other climbers died in the attempt.	1959
Elizabeth Knowlton	The United States	She was a member of the joint German-American climb to Nanga Parbat, in the Himalayas.	1932
Hettie Dyhrenfurth	The United States	She reached the top of Queen Mary Peak in the Himalayas and gained the world altitude record for women.	1934

Students can work individually, in pairs, or in groups to answer questions 1–5.

Answers: 1. Alexandra David-Neel's journey was remarkable because no other man or woman had disguised himself or herself in order to make the long journey to the forbidden city of Lhasa. 2. A "suffragette" was someone who campaigned for women's rights (specifically the right to vote) in the nineteenth century.

Answers to questions 3 through 5 will vary.

Thinking Critically

Elicit or explain the definition of predicting as a critical thinking skill. Have students read the information on **predicting** in the box on page 29 and complete the predictions chart in pairs or groups. Have them share their charts with the class. Afterwards, ask students how they might apply prediction to other types of readings. They can use this critical thinking school to ask questions and make guesses about future events to be related in an article or a story, and then see if the author fulfilled those predictions. If the author does not address the issues that the students predicted might be addressed, students might then ask themselves what the effect of this omission is. Should the author have addressed these issues? Does the omission seem intentional or unintentional? How might the text have been different if those issues had been addressed?

Freewriting

5 Page 29.
Remind students that the purpose of freewriting is to generate ideas on the page, and that they should not worry about grammar, spelling, accuracy, or even complete sentences. The purpose is to just keep writing. The writing from this particular Activity can be used later to help them with Part 2 Activity 5 on Student Book page 31.

Gathering Information

6 Page 29.
Have students use the Internet or the library to research an explorer of their choice. The

information they find will be used for an oral presentation (Activity 7). Encourage them to find at least one picture of the explorer. If they cannot, perhaps they can find pictures of the region in which the person traveled. Note that this information can be recycled for Part 2 Activity 4 Student Book page 31, which asks students to write a paragraph about the person they researched.

7 Page 30.
Have students organize their notes into outline form for the presentation. Allow time for them to practice their presentation and then have them present to the class.

Part 2 Language for Writing

Describing Explorers

1 Page 31.
Explain to students that they can use these vocabulary words for their own writing and discussion activities in this chapter, and specifically in the subsequent writing activities 3–6 on page 31). If they are keeping a vocabulary log in this course, encourage them to add these words. Have students discuss the meanings or guess the meanings in pairs first; then have them use the dictionary to check their definitions.

2 Page 31.
The words on this list are synonyms of the words in the chart above. Have students find the synonym for each example and write out the sentences in which the words appear. Have them identify the part of speech of the words that correspond to those in the list.

Answers:
Line 1: distant = remote (adjective)
Line 2: climb to the top = ascend (verb)
Line 7: one of the first people to do this = a pioneer (noun)

Line 12: hide one's identity = disguise oneself (verb)

Line 14: not permitted = forbidden (adjective)

Line 17: strong-willed = ardent (adjective)

Line 34: journeys to explore = expeditions (noun)

Line 39: mountain-climbers = mountaineers (noun)

Line 50: famous, notable = remarkable (adjective)

3 Page 31.

Have students choose an explorer from the chapter that interests them and incorporate the new vocabulary words into a paragraph about him or her. Remind students to include a topic sentence. Students can proofread each other's paragraphs in pairs before handing them in to you, checking in particular for correct use of new vocabulary words. As a twist on this activity, students could leave out the explorer's name when they write the paragraph. Other students could then guess the explorer based on the clues provided in the paragraph. This approach would force students to be as specific as possible in their descriptions.

4 Page 31.

Have students return to their notes and presentation outline from Part 1 Activities 6 and 7 Student Book pages 29–30. Have them incorporate new vocabulary words and a topic sentence as they restructure their notes into a coherent paragraph. As with the previous activity, students could proofread each other's paragraphs in pairs, checking specifically for correct use of vocabulary.

5 Page 31.

If students have difficulty thinking of a noun to describe a characteristic of an explorer, you might encourage them to think of an adjective first and then find the noun form. As a brainstorming activity, students could list possible nouns and/or adjectives first, and then select what they feel is the most important. They might also look back at their freewriting activity on page 29 for ideas. The example they provide to illustrate this characteristic could be from an explorer mentioned in the book, in their own or a peer's research presentation, or from some other source. As with the previous two activities, students could proofread one another's paragraphs, checking specifically for correct use of vocabulary.

6 Page 31.

If students did a brainstorming activity for the previous activity (listing adjectives/nouns to describe explorers), those notes might be useful for planning this activity; students could choose several words from their list. As with the previous activities, students could proofread one another's paragraphs, checking specifically for correct use of vocabulary.

Part 3 Systems for Writing

The Thesis Statement: Topic and Angle

First elicit what students may already know about thesis statements. Then have them read the information in the boxes on page 32 and discuss the example thesis statement below. Have students identify the supporting ideas that an essay from the sample thesis statement would develop. (Supporting idea 1: books by explorers were entertaining; Supporting idea 2: books by explorers were educational). Depending on your particular class needs and comfort level, you might type up some anonymous examples of students' thesis statements from the essay or essays they wrote in Chapter 1 and have students evaluate their effectiveness. If you do this, keep in mind that some students may feel insecure about having their writing singled out, even anonymously. Reassure them that the examples are intended merely to demonstrate common challenges and successes that writers face when writing a thesis statement; they are not examples of "bad" writing.

1 Page 32.

Have students work individually, in pairs, or as a class to identify the topic and angle of the thesis statements.

Answers:

1. Topic: The urge to discover. Angle: The origins of that urge: first wanting to find how to live, and later wanting to find how to have fun.

2. Topic: The motivation to explore new lands. Angle: The reasons for that motivation, which are a thirst for adventure and a desire to know.

3. Topic: Alexander the Great was one of the world's greatest explorers. Angle: The reasons why he was one of the world's greatest explorers: he and his men solved many mysteries about geography and weather.

2 Page 33.

Have students read the students predict the way an essay would develop from the third thesis statement.

Answer: The writer will explain what mysteries about geography and weather were solved by Alexander the Great on his journeys.

Supporting Ideas

Have students read the information in the box on page 33, as well as the explanations of criteria for supporting ideas in Activity 3. You may wish to point out that depending on how the thesis statement is phrased, the angle and supporting ideas might come before the topic, or vice versa. Notice in number 1, with the example under **degree of generality** or specificity, the supporting ideas appear first in the sentence.

3 Page 33.

Have students return to the thesis statements on Student Book page 21 and identify the supporting ideas.

Answers: 1. wanting to find how to live, wanting to find how to have fun 2. a thirst for adventure, a desire to know 3. mysteries about the earth's geography, mysteries about the earth's weather.

4 Page 35.

Have students work in pairs to discuss and rewrite the erroneous thesis statements. Encourage them to refer back to the three criteria for supporting ideas and explain the reason for the problem.

Answers:

1. What's wrong: the ideas are not distinct. Sample rewrite: Space exploration and undersea exploration have two things in common: both are motivated by the desire to learn more about the world and concerns about the environment.

2. What's wrong: the ideas do not have the same degree of specificity; the first idea is general and the second is too specific. Sample rewrite: Yuri Gagarin's single orbit of the earth on April 12, 1961, was newsworthy because the Russian cosmonaut was the first man to travel in space and he completed the journey alone.

3. What's wrong: the ideas do not have the same degree of importance in relation to the topic. Sample rewrite: Although Alan Shepard and Yuri Gagarin represented different countries, their early flights in space paved the way for future Russian-American space projects and increased our knowledge of humans' ability to live in space.

5 Page 36.

Have students work individually or in pairs to evaluate the effectiveness of the thesis statements.

Answers:

1. bad; the supporting ideas are not distinct. Sample rewrite: Edmund Hillary proved himself a courageous and physically

strong mountain climber in 1953 when he ascended Mount Everest.

2. bad; the supporting ideas do not have the same degree of specificity (the first is general, the second is specific). Sample rewrite: From earliest times, humans have been driven by a desire to know the unknown and to improve their quality of life.

3. good

4. bad; the supporting ideas do not have the same degree of importance in relation to the topic. Sample rewrite: Great strides in space exploration were made in 1984, when two American astronauts floated free in space: They gathered some important information about humans' ability to live in space and changed the way that future space explorations could be conducted.

5. bad; no clear supporting ideas, and statement is too specific to be developed in an essay. Sample rewrite: Amelia Earhart's explorations were moving because she was the first woman to fly a plane across the Atlantic and she never returned from her last voyage.

6 Page 37.

Have students use the notes to write a thesis statement about Jacques Cousteau and one about dangers in space. Then have them share their thesis statements with a partner. They should check each other's statements for topic, angle, and supporting points. Remind them to their supporting points for the three criteria. They will need to be selective about what information to include from the notes.

Sample answers: Answers will vary. Jacques Cousteau contributed greatly to undersea explorations because of his two inventions: the aqualung and the bathyscaphe. / Explorers in space face many dangers, primarily the risks of meteors tearing holes in the spaceship and ultraviolet rays causing burns.

Focus on Testing

Planning a Good Thesis Statement

Have students read the information in the box on page 37. You might have them practice prewriting techniques for a thesis statement in a timed essay situation by giving them one of the writing assignments on Student Book page 38 as a timed writing test.

Writing Assignments. Page 38.

Have students choose one of these topics for a writing assignment to complete at home or, alternatively, in class as a timed essay. If you give this as a homework assignment, encourage students to use their freewriting, discussion notes, and paragraph assignments to help them with content for the assignment. Also encourage students to write an outline, thesis statement, and topic sentences before beginning the assignment; you may even wish to have students turn in an outline to you before they do the actual writing, or have students check them in pairs.

Part 4 Evaluating for Rewriting

Allow for plenty of class time for this process of drafting and revising. Students will be evaluating each other's drafts with particular criteria in mind for each stage of this process. Students can conduct peer reviews in a variety of ways, in pairs and small groups, orally and in writing; they may choose their own pairs or be assigned a partner by yourself. You may wish to vary the structure of peer review sessions throughout the course.

Evaluating the First Draft. Page 39.

Have students read the drafts silently and then discuss the general questions with their partner. They may find it useful to take notes on the questions to aid them in discussion.

Evaluating the Second Draft. Page 40.

Step 1 will likely work best if students write their answers, as they are looking for very specific things. Students can show their answers to the author of the paper, or hold a discussion based on their answers. Students can keep the same partner from their peer review of the first draft, or work with a new partner.

Writing the Final Draft. Page 41.

If students are keeping a writing portfolio, have them add the final version of this essay. They can look back on it later to check their progress.

Video Activities: Extreme Sports

Before You Watch

Have students discuss the questions in groups. To facilitate conversation for question 2, you may wish to bring in photos of hangliders or paragliders, if possible. Answers will vary.

Watch [on video]

Play the video. Have students listen for the answers and write them. Play the video again, if necessary. Have students compare their answers in groups.

Answers: 1. a 2. c 3. b

Watch Again [on video]

Play the video. Have students listen for the answers and write them. Play the video again, if necessary. Have students compare their answers in groups.

Answers:
1. Torey Pines
2. a. it = hangliding and paragliding b. the veterans are people who have done this sport many times c. frightening, scary, threatening d. peaceful, serene, joyful
3. a, c, e

After You Watch

You might have students discuss the topic first in their groups in order to help them generate ideas and opinions for their essays. Allow some time for brainstorming/ prewriting activities if possible. Students might list all the dangerous sports they can think of; this activity would give them some specific examples to consider in the essay. You could also have them list possible reasons why people would do these sports. Encourage them to write a thesis statement, outline with supporting reasons, and topic sentences for paragraphs before beginning to write. You could have students hand in outlines and thesis statements first, or have students check them in pairs and give feedback to one another. Or, if time permits, you could type up everyone's thesis statement, anonymously, and have the class evaluate their effectiveness and give suggestions.

Sex and Gender

Goals

- **Research and write about gender differences in communication**
- **Learn ways to develop paragraphs**
- **Edit for the main idea and paragraph development**
- **Recognize and use supporting information from experts**

Part 1 Ideas for Writing

Getting Started

1 Page 44.

Have students look at the pictures and read the captions. Then have them discuss the questions as a class or in groups.

2 Page 45.

Have students work in groups to discuss gender communication differences and their possible causes. Groups could list their ideas and share them with the class.

Reading for Ideas

3 Prereading Questions. Page 45.

Have students discuss the prereading questions in groups. To facilitate conversation for question 3, in case students are not familiar with discussion board postings or online chatting, you could bring in some examples of those types of communication for students to look at, or direct them to appropriate websites. Then have them read the article. You can have them read silently while you read aloud, or you can have them take turns reading each paragraph aloud as a class or in groups.

4 Postreading Questions. Page 47.

Have students answer the questions individually and share their answers with a partner or group.

Answers:

1. Men tend to debate, report, and try to dominate or control the conversation. They often seek solutions to problems or offer advice. They may use fewer intensifiers, make declaratives statements, change topics frequently, speak loudly, and interrupt. Women relate rather than debate, and they seek rapport and cooperation. They try to establish intimacy, discuss problems, and show concern. They usually stick to one topic and don't seek to dominate or control. They tend to use more intensifiers than men, and to make their statements sound like questions.

2. Online, men are usually more assertive, and they tolerate or even enjoy "flaming" and insults. Women, however, tend to be unsure, hesitant, and apologetic. They ask questions. They dislike and avoid "flaming."

Answers to questions 3 through 5 will vary.

Thinking Critically

Elicit or explain the definition of an expert: someone with specialized knowledge about a certain subject. Ask them to give examples of people who are experts (such as people who have academic credentials or who have written well-reviewed books/articles on a topic), versus non-experts (such as ordinary people posting their thoughts on a subject on the Internet). Have students read the information on recognizing supporting information from experts in the box on page 48 and complete the chart in pairs or groups. Encourage them to use a similar chart format when conducting their own research later.

Name	Qualifications	Findings
Jennifer Coates	Wrote *Women, Men and Language*.	In studying men-only and women-only discussion groups, she found women reveal a lot about private lives, stay with one topic, let all speakers complete their sentences, and encourage full participation. Men talk less about personal relationships and feelings and more about current affairs, travel, and sports; they change topics a lot, compete to show information/knowledge, and try to dominate.
Dr. Lillian Glass	Wrote *He Says, She Says: Closing the Communication Gap Between the Sexes*	There are many differences in the way men and women communicate, both verbally and non-verbally. Men speak more loudly, interrupt more often, use fewer intensifiers, and use declarative statements. Women use question intonations.
Susan Herring	She spoke on a panel called "Making the Net 'Work'"	Men are more assertive than women are on discussion boards.
Gladys We	She wrote a graduate research paper entitled "Cross-Gender Communication in Cyberspace."	Her results of a survey of men and women show most people felt gender was not that important online. She thinks online communication has many of the problems of face-to-face communication, but is potentially liberating because of its anonymity.

Freewriting

5 Page 48.

Remind students that the purpose of freewriting is to generate ideas on the page, and that they should not worry about grammar, spelling, or accuracy. The writing from this particular Activity will be used later to in Part 2 Activity 4 on Student Book page 50.

Gathering Information

6 Page 49.

Encourage students to observe gender differences in a variety of media: TV, movies, plays. Encourage them to develop a chart for taking notes and classifying the differences. For example, students could list the differences from the article along one side of a chart, and list the types of media (names of TV shows, movies, etc.) at the top. Note that these notes will be used not only for Activity 7 below, but also in Part 2 Activity 5 Student Book page 50; students will be asked to write a paragraph describing gender communication differences they observed.

7 Page 49.

Put students in groups to compare notes from Activity 6. If time allows, have them write and perform a scene from one of the media observed, or a fictional scene based on the kinds of communication styles they observed.

Part 2 Language for Writing

Discussing Communication Differences

1 Page 49.
Have students work individually or in pairs to locate examples of the connecting words in the article.

Answers:
1. *while* is found in line 28: She also found that <u>while</u> men make more declarative statements, women make statements sound like questions…

2. *on the other hand* is found in line 18: Men, <u>on the other hand</u>, rarely talk about their personal relationships and feelings…

3. *in contrast* is found in line 37: Women, <u>in contrast</u>, tend to hedge (be unsure), apologize, and ask questions.

4. *whereas* is found in line 11: In other words, men often seek direct solutions to problems and useful advice, <u>whereas</u> women tend to try to establish intimacy… *whereas* is also found in line 38: Men also appeared to enjoy, or at least tolerate, "flaming" (insulting others online), <u>whereas</u> women disliked and avoided it.

5. *however* is found in line 46: Furthermore, We thinks that online communication has all the misunderstandings and confusions of face-to-face communication between men and women; <u>however</u>, she feels that it is potentially liberating because people can be anonymous.

2 Page 50.
Explain to students that they can use these vocabulary words for their own writing and discussion activities in this chapter, and specifically in the subsequent writing activities 3–5 on page 50). If they are keeping a vocabulary log in this course, encourage them to add these words. Have students discuss the meanings or guess the meanings in pairs first; then have them use the dictionary to check their definitions.

Answers: 1. varying 2. speech characteristics 3. associated with 4. relate 5. rapport 6. intimacy 7. empathy 8. stick to 9. dominate 10. findings 11. assertive 12. liberating 13. anonymous

3 Page 50.
Have students write descriptive sentences about the photos on Student Book page 44, using as many new words as possible. Then have students share their sentences with the class or a partner and check for correct usage.

4 Page 50.
This activity asks students to make their freewriting activity a formal writing piece. Assure them that they may not need to use everything they wrote when they shape their ideas into a paragraph, and that they may wish to change the order of their ideas. Or, if they like the way their freewriting turned out, they may wish to keep the general structure but polish the grammar and add the new words/expressions where appropriate.

5 Page 50.
Have students return to their notes from Part 1 Activity 6 Student Book page 49. Have them incorporate new vocabulary words and a topic sentence as they restructure their notes into a coherent paragraph. Students can proofread each other's paragraphs in pairs, checking specifically for correct use of vocabulary.

Part 3 Systems for Writing

Paragraph Development

First elicit what students may already know about paragraph development. You might even give them two examples of paragraphs, one thin and under-developed, and one adequately developed, and have students try to describe the differences. Then have them read the information in the boxes.

1 Page 51.

Have students read the paragraph individually and discuss its merits in pairs.

2 Page 52.

Have students work in pairs to answer the questions and develop the paragraph. Then have pairs compare their results with other pairs so they see that there can be more than one way to develop a paragraph.

Sample Answers (possible answers to the questions are in italics):

- One way to learn a foreign language is to watch the nonverbal communication of the native speakers. *Nonverbal communication often conveys just as much as words, and it can vary from culture to culture.*

- Watch how people behave when they talk to each other. *Even if you do not understand the words they are saying, you may understand the basic ideas of the conversation just by watching gestures and facial expressions.*

- Observe the gestures they use and try to figure out what they mean. *For example, in the United States, the hand signal of a thumb and forefinger forming a circle means "okay." However, in Japan this gesture means "money," and in France it means "worthless" or "zero."*

- See if you can tell the difference between man-to-man, woman-to-woman, and man-to-woman speech. *Do you think that men and women speak different languages?*

3 Page 52.

Have students write possible questions individually or in pairs. After students rewrite the paragraph to answer anticipated questions, have them compare revisions with a partner to check if the questions were adequately answered.

Sample Answers (possible reader questions are in parentheses; development/answers appear in italics):

- There are three areas of difference between men's and women's communication styles. (How do you know?) *Researchers who have studied men and women conversing in single-gender groups and mixed groups have identified these areas.*

- One area is using language to dominate versus using it to establish rapport. (Who uses language in these ways, men or women?) *In general, men tend to try to establish domination or control in a conversation, whereas women try to establish intimacy, express concern, facilitate cooperation, and allow everyone to participate.*

- Another area is in the use of declarative statements versus questions. (Who uses language in these ways? What is an example of this tendency?) *Men tend to speak more assertively, while women's statements often come out sounding more like questions in their intonation, or with question tags at the end. For example, a man might say, "It's a nice day." A woman might say, "Isn't it a nice day?" or "It's a nice day, isn't it?"*

- Using and tolerating insults reflects another area of difference. (Who reacts differently in this area? In what situation would insults be used or tolerated?) *In online communication, studies have shown that men are more tolerant of—and may even enjoy—"flaming," or a form of insulting people in online discussion forums. Women, on the other hand, tend to dislike and avoid insulting people online.*

4 Page 53.

This activity is similar to Activity 3 in that it asks students to anticipate questions; however, it allows students to develop the paragraph with ideas from their personal experience. Answers will vary.

Sample Answers (possible reader questions are in parentheses; development/ answers appear in italics):

- A good language learner has three important characteristics. (What are they?) *These characteristics are motivation, aptitude, and goals.*

- First, he or she must be motivated. (Why is motivation important? What is an example of motivation to learn a language?) *An unmotivated student may expect a book or a teacher to spoon-feed the language, when in fact learning a language takes a great deal of effort on the part of the student as well. A motivated student might do things like keep a vocabulary log and a journal, practice using new words and structures in conversation, read a lot, and talk to native speakers as much as possible.*

- Second, he or she should have some language-learning aptitude (basic ability). (Why is aptitude important? What is an example of how aptitude can help?) *If a student has already learned another language, he or she will probably have a general idea of how to learn a foreign language; they may also develop an ear for correct structures and pronunciation. For example, someone with a high aptitude for learning a language might be able to watch a TV show or read a newspaper and use strategies like context clues to guess the general meaning.*

- Finally, the learner should have clear goals. (What are goals important? What are some examples of language-learning goals?) *Learning a new language can be frustrating at times, and if a student lacks goals, he or she*

may not make good progress through the difficult times. If a student has a goal of working or traveling in another country, for example, they may learn more quickly and enthusiastically than someone who is studying a language merely to fulfill an academic requirement.

5 Page 53.

Help students prepare for this writing task by allowing a few minutes for brainstorming. Individually, perhaps in their journals, they could list possible communication differences to write about; they might look back at the reading in this chapter, their freewriting, and their discussion notes. Encourage them to anticipate reader questions and write them down as they are writing the first draft of the paragraph. Have them check their own paragraph for answers before exchanging paragraph with a partner.

6 Page 53.

Have students choose whichever paragraph they like from Part 2, Student Book page 50, and exchange paragraphs with a partner to check for reader questions. Encourage revision to answer the questions.

Focus on Testing

Pretending That You Are the Reader
Have students read the information in the box on page 53. You might have them practice anticipating reader questions in a timed essay situation by giving them one of the writing assignments on Student Book page 54 as a timed writing test.

Writing Assignments. Page 54.
Have students choose one of these topics for a writing assignment to complete at home or, alternatively, in class as a timed essay. If you give this as a homework assignment, encourage students to use their freewriting, discussion notes, and paragraph assignments to help them with content for the assignment. Also encourage

students to write an outline, thesis statement, topic sentences, and anticipated reader questions before beginning the assignment. You may even wish to have students turn in an outline with anticipated reader questions before they do the actual writing, or have students outlines and questions in pairs.

Part 4 Evaluating for Rewriting

Allow for plenty of class time for this process of drafting and revising. Students will be evaluating each other's drafts with particular criteria in mind for each stage of this process. Students can conduct peer reviews in a variety of ways, in pairs and small groups, orally and in writing; they may choose their own pairs or be assigned a partner by yourself. You may wish to vary the structure of peer review sessions throughout the course.

Evaluating the First Draft. Page 55.

Have students read the drafts silently and then discuss the general questions with their partner. They may find it useful to take notes on the questions to aid them in discussion.

Evaluating the Second Draft. Page 56.

Step 1 will likely work best if students write their answers, as they are looking for very specific things. Students can show their answers to the author of the paper, or hold a discussion based on their answers. Students can keep the same partner from their peer review of the first draft, or work with a new partner.

Writing the Final Draft. Page 57.

If students are keeping a writing portfolio, have them add the final version of this essay. They can look back on it later to check their progress.

Video Activities: Seeking Love

Before You Watch

Have students discuss the questions in groups and then share their answers with the class. Answers will vary.

Watch [on video]

Play the video. Have students listen for the answers and write them. Play the video again, if necessary. Have students compare their answers in groups.

Answers: 1. love 2. a, b, c 3. a & b = √ c & d = X

Watch Again [on video]

Play the video. Have students listen for the answers and write them. Play the video again, if necessary. Have students compare their answers in groups.

Answers: 1. a 2. d 3. b, c, e 4. b 5. b 6. a

After You Watch

You might have students discuss the topic first in their groups in order to help them generate ideas and opinions for their essays. Alternatively, you could have them brainstorm ideas individually, and then share a thesis statement and outline with groups. Group members can help each other anticipate reader questions. You may wish to spend some time going over structures for comparison/contrast essays. Students can discuss similarities first and then differences, or they can discuss each aspect of dating in turn, discussing it in terms of the video and their own experience in each paragraph. If any students seem uncomfortable writing about their own dating experiences or personal life, they can write about a friend's experiences, or someone on a television show or in a movie

Mysteries Past and Present

Goals

- **Research and write about a structure or monument from the past**
- **Learn expressions and structures for speculation**
- **Recognize and use different types of supporting material**
- **Use knowledge of word parts to define new words**

Part 1 Ideas for Writing

Getting Started

1 **Page 60.**
Have students look at the pictures and read the captions. Then have them discuss the questions as a class or in groups and report their answers to the class.

2 **Page 61.**
Have students work in groups to complete the know/want to know chart. They will be completing the "L" column later.

Reading for Ideas

3 **Prereading Questions. Page 62.**
Have students discuss the prereading questions in groups. Answers will vary. Then have them read the article. You can have them read silently while you read aloud, or you can have them take turns reading each paragraph aloud as a class or in groups.

4 **Postreading Questions. Page 64.**
Have students answer the questions individually and share their answers with a partner or group.

Answers: 1. They were constructed between 2723 and 2563 B.C. 2. An Egyptologist studies Egypt. 3. The purpose of the Giza Pyramids was to commemorate dead kings. 4. Answers will vary; sample answers: Religion was important to the ancient Egyptians. They valued the sacred in their everyday life. At the same time, they were a practical people, with superior organizational skills. 5. Answers will vary; sample paraphrase for sentence one: Many guesses and theories are made about pyramids. Sample paraphrase for sentence two: The Pyramids' construction has a unique religious meaning. 6. Answers will vary.

Thinking Critically

Write "Egyptologist" on the board and draw a line between "Egypt" and "ologist." Explain that "-ologist" is a suffix (a group of letters attached to the end of a word) that means a type of scientist or student. Elicit other examples of words ending with this suffix (such as biologist, musicologist, geologist, etc.) Explain to students that they can define and remember the meaning of new words more quickly by looking for word parts that have common meanings. Have students read the information on **using your knowledge of word parts** in the box on page 65 and identify word parts and meanings with a partner. Encourage them to list other words they know, or find other words in a dictionary, that use the same word parts: *spec, in, num, prov, det, prog, fun.*

Freewriting

5 **Page 65.**
Remind students that the purpose of freewriting is to generate ideas on the page, and that they should not worry about grammar, spelling, or accuracy.

Gathering Information

6 **Page 65.**
Students may choose one of the monuments pictured at the beginning of this chapter, or

another monument of their choice. Have them do research in the library or on the Internet. Help them focus their research by giving some time in class to discuss and brainstorm ways to narrow the topic. For example, students could focus on the significance of a monument in the past or the present, or both. You might have students write out some research questions or make a Know/Want to Know chart similar to the one they wrote on Student Book page 61. Remind them to record their sources as they research (title, author, publication, date, pages, web site address), as they will be asked to provide bibliographic references at the end of their presentation and they may wish to refer their classmates to certain sources when they answer questions after their presentation.

7 Page 65.

Have students prepare for their presentation by organizing their research notes from Activity 6 into an outline form and deciding what information is essential and supports one main idea. Elicit or give some ideas for writing a "catchy" introduction and getting the audience's interest. For example, they might start with intriguing questions (are there mysteries or legends about this monument?), an anecdote (did the person see the monument in person, or is there a story about someone who did?), a quotation (has someone said something interesting or famous about the monument?), or a picture that they can show and describe. You can also help them to prepare for the question and answer session following their presentation by going through their outline and anticipating audience questions, similar to the way in which they anticipated reader questions in Chapter 3. They could even exchange outlines with a partner and help each other anticipate questions. Allow time for students to practice their presentations and encourage them to speak from notes rather than reading the presentation word for word. Note that students should save their research, presentation notes, and outlines, as they will later be writing a paragraph related to their topic (Part 2 Activity 6 Student Book page 68).

Part 2 Language for Writing

Speculating

1 Page 66.

Discuss the word *speculation* and be sure that all students are comfortable with its meaning. Read the definition under the heading "Speculating" and elicit or give additional examples of when people might use speculation. (For example, theories in the sciences sometimes involve speculation in their early stages; these theories are then tested). Then have students work individually, in pairs, or as a class to locate the two additional sentences that express speculation in the article.

Answers:

2. It has been estimated that the interior and exterior of the Cheops Pyramid are composed of about 2,300,000 separate limestone blocks… (lines 22–24).

3. It is generally thought that here purification ceremonies and mummification took place, and therefore this area was accessible only to priests (lines 56–57).

After students have completed Activity 1, explain that some types of modals and certain expressions are useful in expression speculation. Have students look at the three speculative sentences in Activity 1, identify them, and underline them. (The modals/expressions are: *must have been, It is estimated, it is generally thought*). Then have them read the other examples on Student Book pg. 66-67. Point out the word order when possibly or probably are used: these adverbs come before the main verb (*possibly constitute*) and after modals (*had probably remained*), except when the *be* verb is used. *Possibly* and *probably* come after the *be* verb (*The Great Pyramid is probably one of the oldest structures in the world.*) If time permits, you could have students practice this concept further by stating or writing some speculations with these expressions about the monuments pictured in the beginning of the chapter, or the monument that they presented on in Part 1 Activity 7.

Describing Ancient Structures or Monuments

2 Page 67.

Explain to students that they can use these vocabulary words for their own writing and discussion activities in this chapter, and specifically in the subsequent writing activities 4–7 page 68). If they are keeping a vocabulary log in this course, encourage them to add these words. Have students discuss the meanings or guess the meanings in pairs first; then have them use the dictionary to check their definitions, and finally have them write synonyms/definitions or sketch pictures.

3 Page 68.

Have students work individually or in pairs to rewrite the factual statements as speculations. Encourage them to vary their use of modals and expressions. Answers will vary.

Sample Answers: 1. The first dynastic ruler of Egypt, Menes, must have redirected the Nile River so that early pyramids could be constructed. 2. It is generally thought that Menes and his early successors administered highly centralized political systems. 3. There are many indications that some of the tombs dating from the First Dynasty (3100–2686 B.C.) belonged to kings and members of the royal family. 4. The king was probably surrounded by a large body of counselors and executives.

4 Page 68.

Have students write their speculations about the ancient Egyptians individually. Then have them trade sentences with a partner to check for correct use of modals and expressions of speculation, as well as correct use of new vocabulary words.

5 Page 68.

Have students brainstorm past phenomena first, listing possible ideas for their paragraph. You might encourage them to think about their classmates presentations from Part 1 Activity 7 for ideas. Then have them write the paragraph and exchange paragraphs in pairs to check for correct use of speculation expressions and new vocabulary words.

6 Page 68.

Have students return to their presentation notes or outline from Part 1 Activity 7 to get ideas for this task. Remind them that they will not be able to include all of their information in one short paragraph, so they need to be selective. Have them focus on one aspect and write a paragraph speculating about the life and values of the people who built the monument. Then have them exchange paragraphs in pairs to check for correct use of speculation expressions and new vocabulary words.

7 Page 68.

This activity asks students to choose one of the new words on Student Book pg. 67 and write and extended definition of it. They need not use speculative language for this, although they may find it appropriate at the end of the paragraph. The goal, however, is to provide concrete examples and sufficient explanation for the word to be understood. As a variation, you could have students do this as a guessing game. Have them write the paragraph as a "clue" to a word that is not given. Then students can work in groups to guess each other's words based on the extended definitions.

Part 3 Systems for Writing

Types of Supporting Material

Explain that supporting material/information can help to develop a paragraph. Elicit what students may already know about types of supporting material. Then have them read the information in the boxes on page 69.

1 Page 69.

Have students read the paragraph individually (you could read it aloud while they follow along), and identify the four types of supporting material.

2 Page 70.

Have students work individually to find types of supporting material and complete the chart; then have them compare answers with a partner. After students complete the chart, read the note at the bottom of Student Book page 70 and emphasize that not every paragraph need include each type of supporting material.

Supporting Material from "The Giza Pyramids"	Type: Example, Fact, Statistic, or Anecdote
...the interior and exterior of the Cheops Pyramid are composed of about 2,300,000 separate limestone blocks...	Statistic
They were constructed between 2723 and 2563 B.C. and are located on the left bank of the Nile River outside Cairo, Egypt. (lines 2–4)	Fact
A pyramid is a huge but simple structure to commemorate a dead king. (lines 8–9)	Fact
The dead king had to continue to exist in the afterlife because he became divine... (lines 9–11)	Fact
Actual construction took place only when the Nile flooded... At this time...(lines 13–16)	Fact
It took 100,000 men twenty years to build the Cheops Pyramid... (lines 16–17)	Statistic
During his campaign in Egypt, Napoleon calculated... (lines 27–2)	anecdote
Most of the casing blocks were removed in the Middle Ages... (lines 36–40)	Fact
The ascent, however, is often forbidden... lines 40–42)	Fact
the oasis between the two deserts, the green of the cultivation in the middle of the yellow sand, the city of Cairo... (lines 45–50)	Examples
There was a funerary temple on the east side... (lines 52–53)	Example
These were connected by a covered walkway... (lines 53–55)	Fact

3 Page 71.

Have students work individually or in pairs to identify the types of supporting material in the two paragraphs.

Answers:

a. Example: 1 Fact: 1, 2, 3, 4 Statistic: 3, 4

b. Example: 1 Fact: 1, 2, 3, 8 Statistic: 2, 3
Anecdote: 6

4 Page 72.

Have students read the list of wonders and select two to write about. They may need or wish to do some additional research on the Internet or in the library, though this should not turn into a research paper and all of the information should relate to the main topic of the paragraph. Have students organize their information into a paragraph outline with a topic sentence before writing the paragraph. Encourage the use of speculative language where appropriate, as well as new vocabulary words from Part 2. Have students exchange finished paragraphs to check for correct vocabulary use and overall clarity.

5 Page 73.

Help students prepare for this writing task by allowing a few minutes for brainstorming. They can read the list of natural wonders, add any others they can think of, and then freewrite on what they know about it or make a Know/Want to Know chart. In helping students to choose a topic, you might lead up to the point in the "Focus on Testing" box below that they may write more easily on a topic that is most familiar to them. However, they may need or wish to do a little research on their topic in the library or on the Internet. As with the previous activity, have students organize their information into a paragraph outline with a topic sentence before writing the paragraph. Encourage the use of speculative language where appropriate, as well as new vocabulary words from Part 2. Have students exchange finished paragraphs to check for correct vocabulary use and overall clarity.

Focus on Testing

Choosing a Familiar Topic

Have students read the information in the box. You might have them practice choosing a familiar topic in a timed essay situation by giving them a choice of the writing assignments on Student Book page 54 as a timed writing test. Encourage students to select the topic they are most familiar with and spend a couple of minutes brainstorming and outlining ideas based on their own knowledge.

Writing Assignments. Page 73.

Have students choose one of these topics for a writing assignment to complete at home or, alternatively, in class as a timed essay. If you give this as a homework assignment, encourage students to use their freewriting, discussion notes, and paragraphs they wrote from this chapter to help them with content. Also encourage students to write an outline, thesis statement, topic sentences, anticipated reader questions, speculations, and possible supporting material before beginning the assignment. You may even wish to have students turn in an outline with types of supporting material identified before they do the actual writing, or have students check each other's outlines in pairs.

Part 4 Evaluating for Rewriting

Allow for plenty of class time for this process of drafting and revising. Students will be evaluating each other's drafts with particular criteria in mind for each stage of this process. Students can conduct peer reviews in a variety of ways, in pairs and small groups, orally and in writing; they may choose their own pairs or be assigned a partner by yourself. You may wish to vary the structure of peer review sessions throughout the course.

Evaluating the First Draft. Page 74.

Have students read the drafts silently and then discuss the general questions with their partner. They may find it useful to take notes on the questions to aid them in discussion.

Evaluating the Second Draft. Page 75.

Step 1 will likely work best if students write their answers, as they are looking for very specific things. Students can show their answers to the author of the paper, or hold a discussion based on their answers. Students can keep the same partner from their peer review of the first draft, or work with a new partner.

Writing the Final Draft. Page 76.

If students are keeping a writing portfolio, have them add the final version of this essay. They can look back on it later to check their progress.

Video Activities: Abduction by Aliens

Before You Watch

Have students discuss the question of UFOs in groups and then share their thoughts with the class. Abduct means the same as b, *kidnap*.

Watch [on video]

Play the video. Have students listen for the answers and write them. Play the video again, if necessary. Have students compare their answers in groups.

Answers: 1. a 2. They have large heads (pear-shaped), huge eyes, small and scrawny bodies, perhaps around 3 feet tall. 3. a 4. b 5. b

Watch Again [on video]

Play the video. Have students listen for the answers and write them. Play the video again, if necessary. Have students compare their answers in groups.

Answers: 1. four 2. her sister 3. 1983 4. 3 years 5. John Mack is a professor of Psychology at Harvard Medical School. He wrote the forward to *Secret Life: Many Firsthand Accounts of UFO Experiences*. 6. John Mack believes that these experiences with aliens are real, and that people who have these experiences are often traumatized and need counseling.

After You Watch

You might have students discuss the topic first in their groups in order to help them generate ideas and opinions for their essays. They could take two sides of the issue in the group and debate it, or simply air their opinions and agree/disagree with one another less formally. Alternatively, you could have them brainstorm ideas individually, and then share a thesis statement and outline with groups. Have them identify types of supporting material to use from the video and other sources. Group members can help each other evaluate the types of supporting material, as well as to anticipate reader questions.

Transitions

Part 1 Ideas for Writing

Getting Started

1 Page 80.

Have students look at the pictures of rites of passage and read the captions. Ask them if they can think of other rites of passage, perhaps from their own cultures. Then have them discuss the questions in groups and report their answers to the class.

2 Page 82.

Have students complete the chart with rites of passage from a different culture. (For example, Latin Americans usually have a big celebration for a young woman's fifteenth birthday). Encourage them to think of both ethnic and religious rites of passage. If your class has several students from the same countries, you could have students work in groups according to nationality/region to complete the chart.

3 Page 83.

Have students compare the rites of passage listed on their chart with North American rites of passage and discuss the differences in groups.

Reading for Ideas

4 Prereading Questions. Page 83.

Have students discuss the prereading questions in groups, or write answers individually and then share them in groups. When you discuss question 1, regarding *adolescence*, you may also wish to cover the terms *childhood, middle-aged* and *elderly / seniors*. Students may be interested to learn that some people have different ideas about when these four stages of life begin and end! Then have them read the article. You can have them read silently while you read aloud, or you can have them take turns reading each paragraph aloud as a class or in groups.

Answers: 1. *Adolescence* is the period of change and development into maturity between childhood and adulthood. Another word for an adolescent is *teenager*. 2. Answers will vary; students are likely to say that the photos on pages 80–81 that indicate adulthood are 3, 4, and/or 5.

5 Postreading Questions. Page 85.

Have students answer the questions individually and share their answers with a partner or group.

Sample Answers:

1. No, there is not a clear difference between childhood and adulthood in American culture. Most people experience a period of adolescence in transitioning from childhood to adulthood; in some cases, this period may be prolonged. (Answers to the second part of the question will vary).

2. Social class might cause a variation in the length of adolescence in American culture. A person who needs to work to earn money may begin working during or soon after high school, thus ending their period of adolescence. On the other hand, someone who has enough money and leisure time to further his or her education or delay work will experience a prolonged period of adolescence.

3. A transition that many American adults (particularly men) experience is a mid-life crisis. This usually occurs around age 40 when they realize that they still have many things left to accomplish, or that they have not accomplished all that they wanted to do, and they feel they are running out of time. Women may also experience this transition, but it may occur early, perhaps in their mid-thirties; it may be related to a fear of not having achieved certain goals of their youth, but also a fear of a future in which they are widowed and dependent upon their children.

4. Attitudes toward aging have changed in American culture in recent years in that there are somewhat less rigid ideas about what people should accomplish in different life stages (for example, many women now delay marriage and childbirth into their thirties or beyond), and there is more of a sense of possibility of enjoying meaningful activities and an active life in one's later years, as opposed to waiting to die.

5. Answers will vary.

Thinking Critically

Elicit or give a definition of *sources:* books, magazines, web sites, or other materials consulted for research purposes. Ask students to give examples of some sources they consulted for assignments in previous chapters. Have students read the information on **using sources** in the box on page 86. If the concept of finding and citing sources seems quite new or challenging for your students, you could expand the task at the end of the box; have students find several sources in the library based on bibliographic information that you provide. (You could give them a list of brief quotes and references; these could come from various sources cited in this chapter). They could photocopy the pages on which the quotes appear as a way to "prove" that they have indeed found the reference. Students could do this individually or in pairs.

Freewriting

6 Page 86.

Remind students that the purpose of freewriting is to generate ideas on the page, and that they should not worry about grammar, spelling, or accuracy. You could introduce a preliminary step to the freewriting by having students first write the name of the culture at the top of the page and then list associated rites of passage, or refer back to the chart they completed at the beginning of this chapter. Students could write impersonally about people in general who participate in this rite of passage, or, if applicable, about their own experience. The writing from this particular freewriting activity will be used later in Part 2 Activity 4 Student Book page 89; they may also find it useful for planning several of the writing assignments listed at the end of this chapter.

Gathering Information

7 Page 86.

Have students choose a rite of passage that interests them, as well as a person to interview. Encourage them to add questions of their own to the questionnaire on Student Book page 87. Encourage them also to find visual aids, music, or artifacts related to this rite of passage. Information from the interview will be used for an oral presentation in Activity 8.

8 Page 87.

Have students prepare for their presentation by organizing their research notes from Activity 7 into an outline form (they may use the format of the questionnaire, or a different format) and deciding what information is essential. Encourage them to anticipate audience questions and either include information to answer those questions in the presentation, or be prepared to answer such questions after the presentation. Allow time for students to practice their presentations and encourage them to speak from notes rather than reading the presentation word for word. Note that students should save their research, presentation notes, and outlines, as they will later be writing a paragraph related to their topic (Part 2 Activity 3 Student Book page 89).

Part 2 Language for Writing

Discussing Rites of Passage

1 Page 88.
Have students work individually or in pairs to locate the synonyms in the article. Explain that they can use these vocabulary words for their own writing and discussion activities in this chapter, and specifically in the subsequent writing activities 3-5 page 89). If they are keeping a vocabulary log in this course, encourage them to add these words and to write them in sentences of their own.

Answers: 1. (physical) maturity 2. festivities
3. betrothed 4. socialization 5. ambiguity
6. prolonged 7. crisis 8. tumultuous
9. turmoil 10. outlive

2 Page 88.
Have students work individually or in pairs to locate other words in the article that have various word forms. Students could use a dictionary to check the word forms. If time permits, encourage them to write sentences using these words in their different forms.

Answers:

Nouns	Verbs	Adjectives
Development	Develop	Developed
Ambiguity		Ambiguous
Confusion	Confuse	Confused
Variation	Vary	Varied
Contribution	Contribute	Contributing
Experience	Experience	Experienced
Realization	Realize	
Conclusion	Conclude	
Excitement	Excite	Excited
Suggestion	Suggest	Suggestive
Inclusion	Include	Included
Dependent	Depend	Dependent
Increase	Increase	Increased

3 Page 89.
Have students return to their presentation notes or outline from Part 1 Activity 8 to get ideas for their paragraph. Remind them that they will not be able to include all of their information in one short paragraph, so they need to be selective. Have them focus on one aspect and write their paragraph, incorporating as many new vocabulary words as possible. Then have them exchange paragraphs in pairs to check for correct word usage.

4 Page 89.
Have students formalize their freewriting from Part 1, incorporating new words and expressions. As with the previous activity, you can have them exchange their work in pairs to check for correct word usage.

5 Page 89.
Have students choose only one of these life stages to be the focus of their paragraph. Allow some time for brainstorming and planning first; they might list the types of changes made, organize them into an outline, and write a topic sentence. Students can exchange completed paragraphs with a partner and check for vocabulary usage.

Part 3 Systems for Writing

Organizing Supporting Material

Review the different types of supporting material by having students tell you what they remember from the previous chapter or from their own writing assignments. Have them briefly discuss challenges they may have faced in deciding how to organize material in a paragraph. Then have students read the information in the boxes. You could even bring in sample paragraphs typed up from past writing assignments and ask students to evaluate the organization and how easy or difficult the paragraphs are to follow. If you do this, the samples should be anonymous. If students seem particularly nervous about their writing, you may wish to forego that approach, or be very reassuring that the samples are merely to illustrate common challenges that writers face, not examples of "bad" writing.

1 Page 90.

Have students read the paragraph individually (you could read it aloud while they follow along), and identify the four types of supporting sentences. You might also wish to have them identify the type of supporting material (fact, example, anecdote, statistic) to reinforce what was learned in the previous chapter.

Answers:
Sentence 1: topic sentence
Sentence 2: bridge sentence
Sentence 3: supporting material (example)
Sentence 4: supporting material (example)
Sentence 5: supporting material (example)
Sentence 6: supporting material (example)
Sentence 7: concluding sentence

Interpreting Supporting Material

Explain that the concluding sentence of a paragraph is usually where the writer interprets or analyzes the supporting material. You might mention that an informal way to think about an interpretation of supporting material is to try to answer the question "So what?" The concluding statement is a place to prove to the reader that the material is important and develops the topic sentence. Have students read the information in the box.

2 Page 91.

Have students work individually (perhaps while you read the paragraph aloud) to notice how the interpretation/concluding statement connects to the supporting material and the topic sentence. Then have them cover up the concluding statement and read the paragraph without it. Have them discuss the effect of each version.

3 Page 91.

Have students work individually or in pairs to identify the types of sentences and supporting material in the two paragraphs.

Answers:
Paragraph 1: sentence 1: topic 2: bridge
3: support (example) 4: support (example)
5: support (example) 6: interpretation
7: concluding
Paragraph 2: sentence 1: topic 2: bridge
3: support (example) 4: interpretation
5: conclusion

4 Page 92.

Answers will vary. Encourage students to use new vocabulary words presented in this section. Have students exchange finished paragraphs to check for correct vocabulary use and overall clarity.

5 Page 92.

Students should use the previous activity as a model for this paragraph writing task; their paragraph should include all the types of sentences as in the previous one, though on a different topic. As with the previous activity, have students exchange finished paragraphs to check for correct vocabulary use and overall clarity.

6 Page 92.

Help students prepare for this writing task by allowing a few minutes for brainstorming. They might list possible transitions to write about, looking back at their freewriting and other writing activities and notes from this chapter. Then they could freewrite on their topic and organize their thoughts into outline form. As with the previous activities, have students exchange finished paragraphs to check for correct vocabulary use and overall clarity.

7 Page 92.

Have students exchange earlier paragraphs they wrote from this chapter and check for all the parts of a paragraph; encourage revision. If students do seem to have all of these parts, encourage them to revise to add more or different kinds of supporting material, or a different interpretation.

Focus on Testing

Editing for Good Organization and Development

Have students read the information in the box. You might have them practice checking for the parts of a paragraph in a timed essay situation by giving them a choice of the writing assignments on Student Book page 93 as a timed writing test. Have them budget time at the end of their writing to check each paragraph to be sure that it has all its parts, and to make any changes if necessary.

Writing Assignments. Page 93.

Have students choose one of these topics for a writing assignment to complete at home or, alternatively, in class as a timed essay. If you give this as a homework assignment, encourage students to use their freewriting, discussion notes, and paragraphs they wrote from this chapter to help them with content. Also encourage students to write an outline, thesis statement, topic sentences, anticipated reader questions, possible supporting material before beginning the assignment. When they write an outline, have them outline the essay as a whole and the individual paragraphs. You may wish to have students turn in a detailed outline before they do the actual writing, or have students check each other's outlines in pairs.

Part 4 Evaluating for Rewriting

Allow for plenty of class time for this process of drafting and revising. Students will be evaluating each other's drafts with particular criteria in mind for each stage of this process. Students can conduct peer reviews in a variety of ways, in pairs and small groups, orally and in writing; they may choose their own pairs or be assigned a partner by yourself. You may wish to vary the structure of peer review sessions throughout the course.

Evaluating the First Draft. Page 93.

Have students read the drafts silently and then discuss the general questions with their partner. They may find it useful to take notes on the questions to aid them in discussion.

Evaluating the Second Draft. Page 94.

Step 1 will work best if students write their answers, as they are looking for very specific things and, in question one, they are essentially writing an outline of their partner's essay. Students can show their answers to the author of the paper, or hold a discussion based on their answers. Students can keep the same partner from their peer review of the first draft, or work with a new partner.

Writing the Final Draft. Page 95.

If students are keeping a writing portfolio, have them add the final version of this essay. They can look back on it later to check their progress.

Video Activities: College Graduation

Before You Watch

Have students discuss the questions in small groups. Allow adequate time to discuss the first question in particular, as students will be writing an essay on a related topic after they watch the video. Answers will vary.

Watch [on video]

Play the video. Have students listen for the answers and write them. Play the video again, if necessary. Have students compare their answers in groups.

Answers: 1. b 2. a 3. c

Watch Again [on video]

Play the video. Have students listen for the answers and write them. Play the video again, if necessary. Have students compare their answers in groups.

Answers: 1. b 2. d 3. a 4. c 5. e

After You Watch

You might have students recall their group discussion of question 1 at the beginning of this activity to get ideas for their essay. Note that this essay assignment is somewhat less formal than ones from previous chapters; they could write this more as a personal essay, using narration and description to take the reader to this specific place and time. If you choose to stress the personal essay form, help students to brainstorm by allowing some prewriting time. You might have them list different senses associated with that time (sights, sounds, smells, tastes, sensations, emotions) to include in the essay. Once students have planned their essay, you could also allow some time for students to relate the story orally in small groups or to a partner; this can help them to focus the essay to include only essential details (especially if you set a time limit), and allows for some preliminary feedback from group members about what additional information they might like and what information seems unnecessary.

The Mind

dreaming tendencies. Have them to write their statements, individually or in groups.

Goals

- **Research and write about an aspect of dreaming**
- **Organize a paragraph according to levels of generality**
- **Edit for the main idea and levels of generality**
- **Learn to interpret symbols**

Reading for Ideas

4 Prereading Questions. Page 100.

Have students discuss the prereading questions in groups, or have them write answers individually and then share them in groups.

Answers: 1. Answers will vary. 2. Sigmund Freud was a nineteenth and early-twentieth century psychologist from Austria. He claimed that dreams revealed things about the unconscious part of our mind.

Part 1 Ideas for Writing

Getting Started

1 Page 98.

Have students look at the pictures related to dreams and answer the questions individually. Then have them share their answers in groups. Did some students interpret or react very differently to the same pictures? Have students report similarities and differences to the class.

2 Page 99.

Have students interview another student about dreams and take notes.

3 Page 99.

Have students work together, in large groups or as a class, to tabulate the results of everyone's interviews. They could do this by making a big chart on the board, listing the questions, and entering their responses from their interviews. Or groups could tabulate their results together and give you their results; you could then type up and distribute the statistics for the class. Have students use this data to answer the questions and make some generalizations about the class's

5 Postreading Questions. Page 102.

Have students answer the questions individually and share their answers with a partner or group.

Sample Answers:

1. Before the twentieth century, people believed that dreams were messages from the gods, visits from demons, or results of a reduced oxygen supply to the brain.

2. Today, one explanation for dreaming is that it is a physiological response to the brain's nighttime activities. Anther explanation is that dreams bring messages from the unconscious.

3. According to the article, three functions of recurring dreams are warnings (or messages) about something in us that needs to be resolved, advice, and predictions about the future. (other functions: alerting us to problems like illness, presenting inner conflicts)

4. A possible explanation of the chandelier dream is that the mother unconsciously gathered information about a dangerous situation (perhaps noticing cracks in the ceiling) and then the dream brought that information to her consciousness.

5. According to the article, recurring dreams mean that information from the unconscious is trying to come to our consciousness, if we can interpret the symbols.

6. According to the article, we should interpret recurring dream symbols by writing down our dreams and thinking of what real-life situations they seem to reflect; we can then identify symbols and what they might mean to us or in that situation. We can also be aware of common symbols, such as clothing, houses, and cars.

Thinking Critically

Students should already be somewhat familiar with the idea of interpretation from the discussion of interpretation sentences in paragraphs that was presented in the previous chapter. Elicit a definition of interpretation. Then have students read the information on interpreting symbols in the box on page 103 and work in groups to offer interpretations of the three dream symbols listed. Have them think of other dream symbols (for example: teeth, airplanes, animals) and possible interpretations. If time permits, and if students enjoy the topic, you could have them collectively put together a dream interpretation guide.

Freewriting

6 Page 103.

By now students should be aware that the purpose of freewriting is to generate ideas on the page, and that they should not worry about grammar, spelling, or accuracy. Note that the writing from this particular freewriting activity will be used later in Part 2, Activity 3, on Student Book pg. 105.

Gathering Information

7 Page 104.

Students can research an aspect of dreaming on the Internet or in the library. Encourage them to write some research questions first, or write a Know / Want to Know chart about their topic. Remind them to record bibliographic information about their sources as they take notes. They should also find or create a visual related to their topic, as they will need to incorporate one into their oral presentation in Activity 8.

8 Page 104.

Have students prepare for their presentation by organizing their research notes from Activity 7 into an outline form and deciding what information is essential. For the last point, a question that helps students relate to the topic, explain that it might be good to begin or end the presentation with this topic to get the interest of the audience. Encourage them to anticipate audience questions and either include information to answer those questions in the presentation, or be prepared to answer such questions after the presentation. Allow time for students to practice their presentations and encourage them to speak from notes rather than reading the presentation word for word.

Part 2 Language for Writing

Interpreting Dreams

1 Page 104.

Have students work individually or in pairs to locate the words in the article. Explain that they can use these vocabulary words for their own writing and discussion activities in this chapter, and specifically in the subsequent writing activities 3–5 Page 89). If they are keeping a vocabulary log in this course, encourage them to add these words and to write them in sentences of their own.

Answers:

1. *to reflect* appears in line 80: "Cars, too, can *reflect* your life..."; here to *reflect* means to provide a mirror to your life, to show something that already exists.

2. *to symbolize* appears in line 85: "To her, the car *symbolizes* freedom and independence..."; here symbolizes means stands for/represents.

3. *to represent* appears in line 79: "Houses may *represent* your perception of your life." Here represent means stand for/symbolize.

4. *To dream of (about) something* appears in line 35: "A woman who frequently *dreams* of being chased by men..." and in line 42: "...one woman who kept *dreaming about* a chandelier falling..."; here it means, literally, dreaming; the prepositions can be used interchangeably and they do not change the meaning.

5. *to have a dream about something or someone* (Exact wording not in the article.) It means to think about someone or something while you are sleeping.

6. *to recur* appears in line 37: "Until she masters her anxiety, her dreams will *recur*." Here it means to happen again and again.

7. *to decipher* appears in line 68: "*To decipher* them, she suggests writing a description..."; here it means to understand/figure out/interpret.

8. *to interpret* Exact wording is not in the article, but *interpreting* appears in line 78: "When *interpreting* repetitive dreams, watch for common symbols." Here it means deciphering or explaining the meaning of repetitive dreams.

9. *a dream image* appears in line 51: "The *image* was either precognition or just an educated guess." It means an visual representation of something.

10. *a symbol* appears in line 34: "...they present that view through metaphors and *symbols*." It also appears in lines 62, 63, and 78. It means something that represents or stands for something else, usually an idea.

11. *the unconscious* appears in line 31: "...'the royal road,' as Freud wrote, to the *unconscious*"; it means the deepest self, or the part of our brain that collects information that we do not thinking about while we are awake.

12. *a metaphor* appears in line 34: "...they present that view through *metaphors* and symbols." It means figurative language that makes a connection between seemingly disparate things.

13. *recurring* appears in line 7: "...millions of people have *recurring* dreams." It also appears in lines 14, 41, 56, 57, 58, and 62. It means repeating over and over.

14. *traumatic* appears in line 11: "Often the dreams have *traumatic* plots." It means very frightening.

15. *unconsciously* appears in line 36: a woman "may *unconsciously* want closeness to a man but be afraid." It also appears in line 46. It means below her state of consciousness, in a way that she is not aware of.

2 Page 105.

Have students write a paragraph interpretation of a work of art individually and then exchange paragraphs with another student to check for correct usage of new words.

3 Page 105.

Have students return to the dream they described in their freewriting and formalize it by correcting grammar, streamlining the information into one paragraph, and using new vocabulary. Have students exchange paragraphs in pairs to check for correct word usage. To expand this activity, you could have students then write an interpretation of each other's dreams.

4 Page 105.

Encourage students to use the new vocabulary words in their oral interpretations. If time permits, and if you feel your students need more practice, have them write up their interpretations in paragraph form after their discussion.

Answers will vary.

Part 3 Systems for Writing

Paragraph Organization: Levels of Generality

Review the basic principles of paragraph organization by having students tell you what they remember from the previous chapter or from their own writing assignments. Then have them read the information in the boxes and study the two methods of organization: top-down and divided. Ask them to consider and discuss the possible advantages and disadvantages of each method, or for what types of writing they might choose one form over another. For example: a very complex topic might need to be broken down as simply as possible; for that reason, the top-down approach might work best.

1 Page 108.

Have students work individually or in pairs to outline the ideas in a general-to-specific pattern.

Answers:
1. Dream interpretation: literal or symbolic
   2. Dream of someone or something in real life—literal
      3. Example—dream of one's mother or friend
   2. Dream of someone or something not found in one's day-to-day life—symbolic
      3. Example—dream of a dragon or some other fantastic animal

2 Page 108.

Have students read the paragraph individually (perhaps while you read it aloud). Then have them answer the questions individually or in pairs.

Answers: 1. The topic is dream interpretation: literal or symbolic 2. The idea is general. 3. The idea expressed in Sentence 2 is that dream images can be literal. This idea relates to the idea of the first sentence in that it gives more specific information about the topic; it forms the first part of the topic sentence. 4. Sentence 4, like Sentence 2, gives more specific information about the topic. It is the second part of the topic sentence. 5. Sentences 3 and 5 give very specific examples to support the two parts of the topic sentence. 6. Sentence 6 is a concluding sentence.

Focus on Testing

"Drawing" Your Ideas

Point out the indentations in the various outlines in this section. Ask students if they have used other methods of diagramming or charting ideas; elicit examples by having students draw some sample sketches, diagrams, or charts on the board. Have students read the information in the box. Encourage them to use some sort of visual depiction or outline to plan their writing in a timed-essay situation. You might reinforce this concept when you assign one of the writing assignments on Student Book page 112.

3 Page 110.

Have students read the paragraph once first for overall comprehension. Then have them work individually to assign the sentences numbers to show levels of generality, and have them compare answers with a partner.

Answers: Sequence of numbers: 1, 2, 3, 4, 2, 3, 4, 2, 1

4 Page 110.

Have students use the outline on Student Book pg. 107 to write their paragraph. More advanced students or students who seem comfortable with the structure may wish to make the assignment more challenging by adding some additional information. They can obtain ideas by discussing the topic with another student or perhaps by doing a quick Internet search using "Physical Anthropology" and "Cultural Anthropology" as key words. Have students exchange completed paragraphs to check for correct vocabulary use and overall clarity.

Sample Paragraph:

The field of anthropology can be divided into two branches: physical anthropology and cultural anthropology. Because people often think that anthropology is the study of other cultures, physical anthropology may be the lesser-known of the two branches for people who are unfamiliar with the field. Physical anthropology involves the study of primates. For example, the great apes, which often seem very human-like, are the subject of numerous behavioral studies. The other branch, which perhaps comes to mind more readily for most people, is cultural anthropology. Cultural anthropology involves the study of other cultures, in areas such as linguistics. For example, many studies are devoted to understanding and cataloguing various Native American languages, many of which are passed on orally and have no written record. Both physical and cultural anthropologists are involved in the important work of understanding different kinds of societies and helping to preserve them.

5   Page 111.

Help students prepare for this paragraph-writing task by allowing a few minutes for brainstorming. They might list possible folk beliefs or sayings to write about, and then choose which would be the most interesting to write about. Then they could freewrite on what they know about their topic. Next, they can organize their thoughts into the two different outlines, and then write the paragraph in two different ways. As with the previous activities, have students exchange finished paragraphs to check for correct structure, vocabulary use, and overall clarity. Have them stay with the same partner to discuss the different effects of the two outlines.

6   Page 112.

Students may choose a paragraph from a finished essay in their portfolio, or a draft of an essay in progress, if they are already working on one of the writing assignments listed at the end of this chapter. Have students try to diagram it according to both outlines, if possible. If they are lacking some information, they should add it until the outlines are complete and then rewrite the paragraph.

Writing Assignments. Page 112.

Have students choose one of these topics for a writing assignment to complete at home or, alternatively, in class as a timed essay. If you give this as a homework assignment, encourage students to use their freewriting, discussion notes, and paragraphs they wrote from this chapter to help them with content. Have students write out a thesis statement, topic sentences, anticipated reader questions, possible supporting material before beginning the assignment. When they write their outline, encourage them to make sketches, diagrams, and charts in addition to the standard outline form, to play with different ways of organizing ideas and find out what works best for them; have them outline the essay as a whole and the individual paragraphs. You may wish to have students turn in a detailed outline before they do the actual writing, or have students check each other's outlines in pairs.

Part 4 Evaluating for Rewriting

Allow for plenty of class time for this process of drafting and revising. Students will be evaluating each other's drafts with particular criteria in mind for each stage of this process. Students can conduct peer reviews in a variety of ways, in pairs and small groups, orally and in writing; they may choose their own pairs or be assigned a partner by yourself. You may wish to vary the structure of peer review sessions throughout the course.

Evaluating the First Draft. Page 112.

Have students read the drafts silently and then discuss the general questions with their partner. They may find it useful to take notes on the questions to aid them in discussion.

Evaluating the Second Draft. Page 113.

Step 1 will work best if students write their answers, as they are looking for very specific things and, in question one, they are essentially writing an outline of their partner's essay. Students can show their answers to the author of the paper, or hold a discussion based on their answers. Students can keep the same partner from their peer review of the first draft, or work with a new partner.

Writing the Final Draft. Page 114.

If students are keeping a writing portfolio, have them add the final version of this essay. They can look back on it later to check their progress.

Video Activities: Social Phobia

Before You Watch

Have students discuss the questions in small groups.

Answers: 1. b 2. answers will vary

Watch [on video]

Play the video. Have students listen for the answers and write them. Play the video again, if necessary. Have students compare their answers in groups.

Answers: 1. social phobia 2. a 3. b

Watch Again [on video]

Play the video. Have students listen for the answers and write them. Play the video again, if necessary. Have students compare their answers in groups.

Answers: 1. b 2. c 3. c 4. b 5. c 6. b 7. c 8. a

After You Watch

Note that this essay assignment is somewhat less formal than ones from most of the other chapters. Students could write this more as a personal essay, using narration and description to take the reader to this specific place and time. If you choose to stress the personal essay form, help students to brainstorm by allowing some prewriting time. First have them list possible events to write about, perhaps according to different ages or phases in their lives, or different places. Then have them choose one they feel most comfortable with or interested in writing about. You might have them list different senses associated with that time (sights, sounds, smells, tastes, sensations, emotions) to include in the essay. Once students have planned their essay, you could also allow some time for students to relate the story orally in small groups or to a partner; this can help them to focus the essay to include only essential details (especially if you set a time limit), and allows for some preliminary feedback from group members about what additional information they might like and what information seems unnecessary.

Working

Part 1 Ideas for Writing

Getting Started

1 Page 118.

Have students look at the pictures and answer the questions in groups or pairs.

Sample Answers:

Question 1 (Describing what people are doing): 1. cultivating plants 2. manufacturing coats 3. conducting an international business meeting 4. attending an ESL class 5. working on a construction site

Question 2 (discussing possible communication problems): 1. The workers might not know specialized names for the plants or for different parts of the plants. 2. The boss and the employees might have communication problems about hours or wages.
3. The businesspeople might have cultural differences in the way they present ideas or make decisions. 4. The students might have difficulty understanding the teacher. / The teacher might have difficulty understanding the

students or helping students who are from a variety of linguistic and cultural backgrounds.

2 Page 119.

Have students answer the questions individually and then compare their answers in pairs or groups. If time permits, you could extend the discussion by having students give reasons to support their opinions and debate the issues informally.

Reading for Ideas

3 Prereading Questions. Page 120.

Have students discuss the prereading questions in groups, or have them write answers individually and then share them in groups. Answers will vary. Then have them read the article. They can read it silently, perhaps while you read it aloud, or they can take turns reading the paragraphs out loud.

4 Postreading Questions. Page 123.

Have students answer the questions individually, in pairs, or in groups. For number 5, put students in groups to try to reach a consensus about one or all of the topics listed. Encourage them to discuss the process of trying to reach consensus; you could even have them write about it in their journals.

Sample Answers:

1. Answers will vary; encourage students to give supporting reasons from the text to support their opinion about how correctly Lanier portrayed the two cultures.

2. The Japanese decision-making process appears to be very slow because decisions are made based on consensus building, and new plans are always discussed at length and decided from below first. Everyone has a chance to discuss a new plan, and to make suggestions. When a decision is finally reached, most people are satisfied with it and knowledgeable about it. Americans,

on the other hand, make their decisions from the top down. The decisions are made more quickly; however, delays can happen later because people at lower levels must be educated about a decision and persuaded to adopt it. Often there is resistance at lower levels because people do not feel that they were consulted during the process and thus are not happy with some aspects of the plan.

3. Answers will vary. Students can write their answers hypothetically, or imagine that they are writing in the voice of a Japanese businessperson.

4. Answers will vary. Encourage students to find concrete examples.

Thinking Critically

Elicit or give a definition of *inference* (a guess, based on material that is provided). (If students have difficulty understanding this concept, you could give a more concrete example: imagine that you go home and find your home a mess, drawers opened, valuables missing, a window broken. Based on the evidence that you see, you can *infer* that you have been robbed). Then have students read the information on **making inferences** in the box on page 124 and work in pairs to complete the chart.

Sample Answers:

Freewriting

5   **Page 124.**

By now students should be aware that the purpose of freewriting is to generate ideas on the page, and that they should not worry about grammar, spelling, or accuracy. If students choose to write about difficulties in doing business in a foreign country, they could write from personal experience or hypothetically; they could even take on a fictional persona. Note that the writing from this particular freewriting activity will be used later in Part 2 Activity 3 Student Book page 125.

Gathering Information

6   **Page 124.**

Read through the interview questions with your students and be sure that they understand what is being asked in each one (some of the vocabulary may be unfamiliar). Encourage students to add questions of their own. You can match students with businesspeople to interview, or have them find people on their own, depending on the resources available and the comfort level of your class. You might want to have students role-play their interviews in class first, with a partner, to practice their interviewing skills (including beginning and ending an interview, taking notes, and asking follow-up questions). Encourage them to take good notes, as

	Ringi	**American Decision-Making Process**
Advantages	Everyone is informed and reasonably satisfied by the time a decision is made.	The decision-making process can appear to go fairly quickly, since a limited number of people are involved in it.
Disadvantages	Delays that result from involving so many people can be frustrating and and confusing to people from other cultures.	Not everyone is happy with the decision that is made; they may feel uninformed or as though their opinion does not count because they were not consulted.

they will need them to prepare for their presentation in Activity 7. If your students desire extra practice conversing with native speakers, you could encourage them to interview several people, if possible.

7   Page 124.

Have students prepare for their presentation by organizing their research notes from Activity 7 into an outline form and deciding what information is essential. They may wish to use the questionnaire itself as an outline. They could present their own opinion about ensuring a successful business, incorporating the remarks of the person they interviewed, or they could present the opinion as that of the interviewee. Encourage them to anticipate audience questions and either include information to answer those questions in the presentation, or be prepared to answer such questions after the presentation. Allow time for them to practice their presentations and encourage them to speak from notes rather than reading the presentation word for word.

Part 2 Language for Writing

Describing Work in a Multicultural Setting

1   Page 125.

Have students work individually or in pairs to locate the words in context in the article. Explain that they can use these vocabulary words for their own writing and discussion activities in this chapter, and specifically in the subsequent writing activities 3–5 on page 89. If they are keeping a vocabulary log in this course, encourage them to add these words and to write them in sentences of their own.

Answers: 1. management style 2. pass the word 3. implement 4. on high 5. sensitive 6. deliberation 7. bargaining 8. initiated 9. harmonious 10. lessened 11. refinements

Describing Causes and Effects

2   Page 125.

Have students read the expressions for causes and effects. You could elicit additional examples of causes and effects by going around the room and having students state them using the expressions. The examples you elicit could be on the topic of the article, or on another topic related to working.

3   Page 125.

Have students return to their freewriting and formalize it by correcting grammar, streamlining the information into one paragraph, and using new vocabulary. Have students exchange paragraphs in pairs to check for correct word usage. Note that this paragraph will be revised again in Part 3, Activity 7, Student Book pg. 130.

4   Page 125.

Have students return to their interview and/or presentation notes from Part 2 Activities 6 and 7. Have them write one or two paragraphs, incorporating as many new vocabulary words and cause/effect expressions as possible. Have students exchange paragraphs in pairs and check for correct usage and overall clarity.

5   Page 125.

Help students brainstorm for this activity first by having them list possible cultural misunderstandings in a business or educational system. They can return to the pictures and questions at the beginning of this chapter for ideas, and add any new situations and problems they can think of. Then have them choose one situation to focus on in the paragraph; have them incorporate as many new words and expressions as possible. Then have students exchange paragraphs in pairs and check for correct usage and overall clarity.

Part 3 Systems for Writing

Cause and Effect

Have students read the information in the boxes on page 126 and study the two types of causal relationships. Ask them if they can think of situations or topics where a simple causal relationship might be the most appropriate, and where a complex one might be the most appropriate.

1 Page 126.

Have students work individually or in pairs to list the causes and effects in the example sentences.

Causes	Effects
Can lead to	that can result in

OR:?

Causes	Effects
The rise in global business	has increased the need to understand cultural interactions within organizations
A lack of knowledge about cross-cultural negotiations can lead to	misunderstanding in a business transaction
Misunderstanding in a business transaction	can result in loss of profits in the long run

2 Page 127.

Have students work individually, in pairs, or in groups to complete the causal chains. Alternatively, you could extend this activity by going around the room and making the chain as long as possible. Students could do that orally or by passing around a piece of paper for each topic and adding causes and effects in turn; all four topics could start at different points in the circle and circulate at the same time. Students could

complete the chains in phrases, building on the examples, or you could have them state or write complete sentences.

Sample Answers:

1. don't pay attention in class—can't complete homework—fail the course—drop out of school

2. try a new sport or activity—be willing to take risks—participate in even more new things—become very good at something you never thought you would try

3. Study English in North America—become proficient—getting a job in an American company—Get a visa and stay for an extended period of time, or permanently

4. take a language class—be self-motivated and hard-working—travel to another country to live—learn to speak the foreign language fluently.

Causal Chain Essay Organization I

Have students read the information in the box on page 128 and the sample outline and thesis below. Emphasize the fact that there must be enough intermediate steps in the causal to chain to form the subject of an entire essay. You may wish to add that if intermediate steps are not mentioned or explained, students run the risk of a logical fallacy called "slippery slope" reasoning: the idea that one event will inevitably and rapidly lead to another. This often happens when the effect predicted is very negative. For example, to prove the assertion "Using e-mail at work will cause you to lose your job," you would need to outline the other causes and effects in between, such as using e-mail for personal reasons, using e-mail frequently on the company's time, letting your own work suffer, and missing deadlines.

Causal Chain Essay Organization II

Have students read the information in the box on page 129. Then have students work individually or in pairs to outline the intermediary steps for an essay that tells the final result in the thesis.

Sample Answer: John's lack of knowledge about Japanese business styles—eads to his impatience at perceived delays—leads to his pressuring Japanese businessmen for information about the decision—leads to his pressuring top executives to make a decision—leads to his offending his Japanese colleagues—leads to his growing extremely frustrated—leads to his resignation from his job.

Focus on Testing

Having a Repertoire of Organizational Patterns

Have students read the information in the box. Elicit other examples of organizational patterns they know from previous chapters or previous experiences (for example: compare/contrast, chronological narrative). Encourage them to choose from a variety of outlining possibilities to plan their writing in a timed-essay situation. You might reinforce this concept when you assign one of the writing assignments on Student Book page 130–131.

4   Page 130.

This activity could also be done in writing, by passing a paper around the room. As with Activity 2, students could state the causes and effects either in phrases (as in the example) or in complete sentences.

Sample Answer: Traveling to another country—gives you firsthand experience with another culture—gives you the confidence to travel to new places—gives you practicing using a foreign language—enables you to gain proficiency in the target language—looks good on your resume and may interest potential employers...

5   Page 130.

Students can write their thesis statements individually and compare them in groups or pairs. They can "test" their thesis by trying to outline the essay from it without looking back at the essay.

Sample Answer: American and Japanese businesses have different decision-making processes, which can frustrate people who are unaware of this important cultural difference.

6   Page 130.

Have students work individually or in pairs to develop outlines and thesis statements for each cause or effect. Stress the importance of writing the outline first; because the causal relationships will be complex, they will not want to include all of the intermediary steps in the thesis statement.

Sample Answers:
1. Outline: Ben attends Spanish class every day—He learns Spanish quickly—He advances to higher-level classes—He applies to a study-abroad program in Spain—He is awarded a scholarship—He spends a semester studying in Spain. Thesis: Ben's regular attendance in Spanish class was the first of many factors that led to his participating in a study abroad program in Spain.

2. Outline: Rica began learning English at a young age, but conversation was never part of the curriculum—the curriculum emphasized grammar and test-taking skills—her teachers were not native English speakers—she traveled a couple of times to North America but was very shy about practicing her English—Rica understands English grammar but cannot speak English. Thesis: Because conversation was not a major component of Rica's experiences learning English, today she understands English grammar but cannot speak the language.

3. Outline: David Livingstone felt very comfortable traveling alone in the African wilderness—He ventured out on his own and traveled to small villages—he met people in the villages—he learned to speak their language—he learned what issues concerned them—when he returned to the U.S., he applied for a job with a nonprofit organization devoted to helping people in Africa—he immediately was

offered the job and was sent back to Africa to work. Thesis: Because of his comfort level, experiences, and knowledge of the African wilderness, David Livingstone had no difficulty obtaining a job with a nonprofit organization and returning to Africa to work.

7 Page 130.

Have students return to their formalized freewriting from Activity 3, Part 2. Encourage them to outline it according to both types of cause/effect formats and choose the format they like best. Have students exchange paragraphs in pairs and check to be sure that all intermediary steps are described and used with appropriate cause/effect expressions. You could also have students outline their partner's paragraphs.

Writing Assignments. Page 130.

Have students choose one of these topics for a writing assignment to complete at home or, alternatively, in class as a timed essay. If you give this as a homework assignment, encourage students to use their freewriting, discussion notes, and paragraphs they wrote from this chapter to help them with content. Have students write out a thesis statement, topic sentences, anticipated reader questions, possible supporting material, and an outline before beginning the assignment. When they write their outline, encourage them to try outlining the essay in two different ways, and to list all of the intermediary steps. You may wish to have students turn in a detailed outline before they do the actual writing, or have students check each other's outlines in pairs.

Part 4 Evaluating for Rewriting

Allow for plenty of class time for this process of drafting and revising. Students will be evaluating each other's drafts with particular criteria in mind for each stage of this process. Students can conduct peer reviews in a variety of ways, in pairs and small groups, orally and in writing; they may choose their own pairs or be assigned a partner by yourself. You may wish to vary the structure of peer review sessions throughout the course.

Evaluating the First Draft. Page 131.

Have students read the drafts silently and then discuss the general questions with their partner. They may find it useful to take notes on the questions to aid them in discussion.

Evaluating the Second Draft. Page 132.

Step 1 will work best if students write their answers, as they are looking for very specific things and, in question one, they are essentially writing an outline of their partner's essay. Students can show their answers to the author of the paper, or hold a discussion based on their answers. Students can keep the same partner from their peer review of the first draft, or work with a new partner.

Writing the Final Draft. Page 133.

If students are keeping a writing portfolio, have them add the final version of this essay. They can look back on it later to check their progress.

Video Activities: Telecommuting

Before You Watch

Have students discuss the questions in small groups.

Sample Answers:

Advantages to Workers	Advantages to Employers
*flexibility with their schedule	*save money
* no commute	*greater employee satisfaction

Disadvantages to Workers

*isolation; may feel frustrated
*hard to be self-disciplined
*may fee less part of a team and thus less motivated

Disadvantages to Employers

*workers may be less productive
*hard to monitor workers' progress/activity
*risk of miscommunications without face to face communication

Watch [on video]

Play the video. Have students listen for the answers and write them. Play the video again, if necessary. Have students compare their answers in groups.

Answers: 1. don't have to get dressed for work, save money on dry-cleaning and buying work clothes, no bad traffic, save money not driving to work, can balance work and family life more easily. 2. greater productivity/results out of employees, company saves a lot of money, helps to reduce pollution (by requiring fewer people to drive)

Watch Again [on video]

Play the video. Have students listen for the answers and write them. Play the video again, if necessary. Have students compare their answers in groups.

Answers:
1. a. number of teleworkers in the U.S.
   b. the average mileage a commuter drives in one year
   c. amount of money a company can save in a year if a worker telecommutes one day a week
   d. the annual cost of driving to work
2. c
3. c
4. a
5. c

After You Watch

Help students to brainstorm and organize their ideas by allowing some prewriting time. First have them list possible advantages and disadvantages of telecommuting. Then have choose their position and circle the most important reasons to support it. Then have them rank the reasons in order of importance, perhaps leading up to the most important point; this will be their outline for the essay. Next, have them look at the reasons to support the other point of view (i.e., if they are writing in support of telecommuting, they should study the list of disadvantages they wrote). Have them decide which points to anticipate from the opposite point of view, and how to incorporate them into their own argument to make their point stronger. Once students have planned their essay, you could allow some time for students to state their arguments and supporting reasons in small groups or to a partner for some preliminary feedback.

Breakthroughs

Goals

- **Research and write about breakthroughs in energy sources**
- **Describe a process**
- **Expand the literal meanings of words**
- **Think about and write for a specific audience**

Part 1 Ideas for Writing

Getting Started

1 Page 136.

Have students look at the pictures and captions and answer the questions individually. Then have them share their answers in groups or pairs.

Answers will vary.

2 Page 138.

Have students answer the questions in pairs or groups. If time permits, you could allow some time for students to briefly research each of these energy sources in the library or on the Internet in order to find out some advantages and disadvantages. Note that Part 1 Activity 7 Student Book page 142 asks students to hold a debate about the advantages of one or more sources of energy. If students spend more time learning about these energy sources now, they can reuse their notes for the debate later. Otherwise, they should be sure to hold on to their notes from this activity to add to them later in preparation for their debates.

Sample Answers:

1. wind—advantages: clean (does not harm the environment), renewable; disadvantages: a lot of land is required to build wind turbines; wind turbines can be noisy; turbines can be expensive to maintain; not all regions have good wind resources to produce adequate amounts of useful energy.

2. sun—advantages: clean, renewable, versatile (many uses of solar energy), saves consumers money. Disadvantages: equipment can be expensive; the energy source is diffuse so you need a large amount of solar panels—and thus a large amount of land—in order to produce useful amounts of energy. Low energy production. Equipment can be very expensive.

3. Oil—advantages: low-cost, easy to distribute; disadvantages: not a renewable resource, as oil reserves are limited; many countries, like the U.S., must depend on foreign countries for much of their oil; prices can fluctuate, depending on economic and political circumstances of oil-producing countries.

4. Coal—advantages: low-cost, reliable, easily distributed. Disadvantages—not a renewable resource; not clean—contributes to global warming and acid rain.

5. Nuclear fission—advantages: low-cost to use, will last a long time, can be used anywhere in the world. Disadvantages—can create hazardous waste; nuclear power plants are dangerous and are expensive to build.

6. hydroelectric power: advantages—renewable, low-cost to use, can be used throughout the world, cause relatively minimal environmental impact, create useful levels of energy. Disadvantages—power plants are difficult and expensive

to build; fish and river life can be negatively impacted.

7. geothermal power—advantages: renewable (an unlimited amount of heat can be extracted from the earth), recyclable, available all the time, doesn't require large and expensive structures like solar panels or windmills. Disadvantages— does not produce much power compared with other sources; can be expensive to use; not available or more complicated to use in some locations (most hydrothermal resources of steam and water are only available in the western U.S.).

Reading for Ideas

3 Prereading Questions Page 139.

Have students discuss the prereading questions in groups, or have them write answers individually and then share them in groups. Answers will vary. Then have them read the article. They can read it silently, perhaps while you read it aloud, or they can take turns reading the paragraphs out loud.

4 Postreading Questions. Page 140.

Have students answer the questions individually, in pairs, or in groups. Have them also return to their answers to the prereading questions and see how many they answered correctly.

Answers:

1. The new solar breakthrough in Australia is the new modular inverter, which is placed on a rooftop to generate clean electricity using the pv (photovoltaic) effect.

2. Technical barriers and their associated costs (safety codes, connections, requirements, etc.) are the biggest obstacles to developing solar energy for widespread use.

3. Possible answers: Australia is a significant participant in the global solar energy industry; they have made huge developments in research in far less time and with far less funding compared with other countries.

4. Another project solar power technologists are working to develop is thin-film, pv solar cell technology, to reduce the cost of solar pv panels.

Thinking Critically

Elicit or give a definition of *literal* (an exact meaning of a word; a dictionary definition). Then have students read the information on **expanding the literal meaning of words** in the box on page 141 and work in pairs to define the expressions from context (or to paraphrase the expressions). Tell students that whenever they read they should pay attention to context clues to determine the best meaning of a word or expression.

Sample Answers: 1. become a viable, realistic choice 2. was judged to be safe and to pass (to be in compliance with) required tests / to meet guidelines 3. creates electricity that is environmentally-friendly (does not harm or pollute the environment) 4. Australia has come closer to being a major presence in the industry worldwide. 5. people who are worried about negative effects on the environment

Freewriting

5 Page 141.

By now students should be aware that the purpose of freewriting is to generate ideas on the page, and that they should not worry about grammar, spelling, or accuracy. Students may find it easiest to write first about their response to the article, writing general comments, questions, points they did not understand, points they would like to know more about. They can then write about their opinion of solar energy in general.

Gathering Information

6 Page 141.

Have students work in groups to research breakthroughs with solar energy. They may need to do research in the library or on the Internet.

Remind them to record bibliographic information about their sources as they take notes, and to locate pictures, as they will need to provide both of those things on their informational poster. Encourage them to find information about at least three breakthroughs, and to work together to write a process paragraph about each to include on their poster. Have students present the information on their poster to the class, or display all the posters in the room and have students walk around and compare results, asking questions to various groups if necessary.

7 Page 142.

Students may find it helpful to prepare for this debate by returning to Part 1 Activity 2, where they listed advantages and disadvantages of various energy sources. They could add to this list of information by doing some research in the library or on the Internet. Give students plenty of time to prepare their opening statement, their three major argument and counterarguments, and closing statement. Go over the debate format with them and have groups assign all members a role so that everyone participates equally.

Part 2 Language for Writing

Discussing Energy

1 Page 142.

Have students work in pairs to discuss the meanings of the words and to check dictionary definitions for unknown words. It may help to have them locate the words in context in the article and write the sentences in which the words appear. They could also write sentences of their own using these words. Explain that they can use these vocabulary words for their own writing and discussion activities in this chapter, and specifically in the subsequent writing activities 2-4 on page 143-144. If they are keeping a vocabulary log in this course, encourage them to add these words.

Describing How Things Work

Have students read the list of expressions for describing processes and the structure of the passive voice. Point out that the passive voice can be used in all tenses, but they will primarily use it in present tense to describe processes or scientific information because the information is always true.

2 Page 143.

By now students should have some degree of knowledge about how a solar cell looks and works, based on the article in the chapter and on their additional research about solar power in Part 2 Activity 6. If they did not do Activity 6, you could have them briefly research solar energy on the Internet or in the library. Have them include as many new vocabulary words and expressions for describing processes as possible. Then have them exchange finished paragraphs with a partner to check for correct word usage and overall clarity.

3 Page 143.

Have students return to the notes they took for their posters about breakthroughs in Part 1 Activity 6. They can rewrite a process paragraph, using new words and expressions.

4 Page 144.

Students may need to briefly research the item they choose on the Internet or in the library. You could add a game element to this activity by having students describe the process without naming the item; students can then read their paragraphs aloud and have the other students guess what item is being described. You could also expand the activity by letting students choose any invention to describe, not just the ones on the list.

Part 3 Systems for Writing

Processes

Review with students the various ways to organize a paragraph or an essay that they have learned so far: compare/contrast, narration, cause and effect. Have students read the information in the boxes on page 144 and study the two types of process—organization paragraphs. Ask them to think of examples of topics that would be appropriate for a chronological description, for example, how to build a solar—energy home. Then ask them about topics appropriate for a structural description, for example, what a solar—energy home looks like.

1 Page 145.

Have students exchange finished paragraphs with a partner to check for vocabulary usage, transition expressions for chronology, and overall clarity/accuracy. You can have them test the accuracy by actually trying to follow each other's directions and make a telephone call. Students should identify what elements of their partner's paragraph most contributed to the overall clarity (or lack of clarity) of the process described.

2 Page 145.

Note that for this process paragraph, students will be using a combination of structural and chronological description. You could point this out to them or ask them to read the direction line closely and elicit from them how they should organize the paragraph. They may need to do a little research about the item they choose on the Internet or in the library. Have them exchange finished paragraphs with a partner and check for organization, transition expressions, and clarity.

3 Page 145.

For this writing activity, students can draw on their own areas of expertise; they need not limit themselves to scientific information or mechanical devices. Encourage them to choose in advance whether they will use chronological description, structural description, or both. You can also lead into the subject of the subsequent "Focus on Testing" box by asking students to think about audience. Tell them that thinking about audience (who the readers are) will help them to determine what steps to include and what words they may need to define or explain. For example, an audience who shares a lot of knowledge about the subject will need fewer explanations, descriptions, or definitions, and you can use a lot of technical

terminology with them. However, an audience unfamiliar with the topic will need more explanation, descriptions, and definitions. After students select a topic, have them decide on an audience spend a few minutes freewriting, perhaps in their journal, about their audience. The easiest audience for them to consider would be the other students in the class. They could list what they think the audience may already know about the topic and what they are not likely to know. Have students exchange completed paragraphs in groups or pairs and check for clarity.

Focus on Testing

Considering the Audience

If you have already presented the notion of audience in Activity 3, this information will build on that concept. Have students read the information in the box. Emphasize the fact that levels of formality are also a consideration when writing for different audiences. (To underscore this point, you might have them return to Activity 1 and rewrite the paragraph for someone they do not know, with a higher level of formality). Encourage them to think about audience when they plan their writing in a timed-essay situation; it would be worth their time to jot a few notes about what their audience may or may not be likely to know about the topic. You might reinforce this concept when you assign one of the writing assignments on Student Book page 146.

Writing Assignments. Page 146.

Have students choose one of these topics for a writing assignment to complete at home or, alternatively, in class as a timed essay. If you give this as a homework assignment, encourage students to use their freewriting, discussion notes, and paragraphs they wrote from this chapter to help them with content. Have students write out a thesis statement, topic sentences, anticipated reader questions, possible supporting material, and an outline before beginning the assignment. When they write their outline, encourage them to choose where they might incorporate chronological and/or structural descriptions of a process. You may wish to have students turn in a detailed outline before they do the actual writing, or have students check each other's outlines in pairs.

Part 4 Evaluating for Rewriting

Allow for plenty of class time for this process of drafting and revising. Students will be evaluating each other's drafts with particular criteria in mind for each stage of this process. Students can conduct peer reviews in a variety of ways, in pairs and small groups, orally and in writing; they may choose their own pairs or be assigned a partner by yourself. You may wish to vary the structure of peer review sessions throughout the course.

Evaluating the First Draft. Page 146.

Have students read the drafts silently and then discuss the general questions with their partner. They may find it useful to take notes on the questions to aid them in discussion.

Evaluating the Second Draft. Page 147.

Step 1 will work best if students write their answers, as they are looking for very specific things and, in question one, they are essentially writing an outline of their partner's essay. Students can show their answers to the author of the paper, or hold a discussion based on their answers. Students can keep the same partner from their peer review of the first draft, or work with a new partner.

Writing the Final Draft. Page 148.

If students are keeping a writing portfolio, have them add the final version of this essay. They can look back on it later to check their progress.

Video Activities: Advances in Medicine

Before You Watch

Have students discuss the questions in small groups.

Watch [on video]

Play the video. Have students listen for the answers and write them. Play the video again, if necessary. Have students compare their answers in groups.

Answers: 1. c 2. c 3. b

Watch Again [on video]

Play the video. Have students listen for the answers and write them. Play the video again, if necessary. Have students compare their answers in groups.

Answers: 1. 2 years 2. BDNF 3. pump, implanted, abdomen, catheter, inserted, vertebrae, release, spinal fluid 4. diagnosis 5. optimistic 6. a. mind-boggling b. neurologist c. prolong d. hypothesis

After You Watch

Help students to brainstorm and organize their ideas by allowing some prewriting time. First have them list other medical treatments that they know about (or would like to know more about). They may wish to do some research on the Internet or in the library. Next, have them decide who the audience is and what the audience is likely to know or not to know. After that, have them outline the essay and decide where to use chronological process description, structural process description or both. Once students have planned their essay, they could get together in pairs or groups, talk about their outlines, and get some preliminary feedback. Group members—especially if they are part of the writer's intended audience—can give useful suggestions about other information to include or information that seems unnecessary. Remind students that they may need to incorporate definitions of specialized words that their readers are not likely to be familiar with.

Art and Entertainment

Goals

- **Research and write about an aspect of art**
- **Analyze and describe art**
- **Write effective introductions and conclusions**
- **Learn to apply what you've learned as a critical thinking skill**

Part 1 Ideas for Writing

Getting Started

1 Page 152.

Have students look at the pictures and captions and answer the questions in small groups.

Answers will vary.

2 Page 155.

Have students keep the same groups or meet in new groups to discuss other works of art and their functions, values, and messages. To facilitate conversation, you might bring in postcards or pictures of famous works of art, or encourage students to do so.

Reading for Ideas

3 Prereading Questions. Page 155.

Have students discuss the prereading questions in groups, or have them write answers individually and then share them in groups. Answers will vary. Then have them read the article. They can read it silently, perhaps while you read it aloud, or they can take turns reading the paragraphs out loud.

4 Postreading Questions. Page 157.

Have students answer the questions individually, in pairs, or in groups. Encourage students to use their own words in their answers; they may find it easier to do so if they try to write their answers without looking back at the book. They could discuss the questions first in groups, looking up the information in the article, and paraphrase as a separate step.

Answers:

1. The author rejects these terms because they imply that African art is inferior to European art, when in fact art from the two cultures is evaluated by very different standards.

2. The nine characteristics of African art are as follows: it is usually has a function, as opposed to being merely decorative; it expresses encounters between the invisible and the visible, or life and death; the idea for the shape of art comes from within the artist, as a spiritual impulse; the artist usually has some other primary occupation; art is considered to reflect community values, not individual expression; secret societies use art for ritualistic purposes; it is abstract; it is in harmony with nature; it is accessible to all people in their everyday lives. Answers to the second part of the question, inviting comparisons to other cultures, will vary.

3. Copying another artist's work in African cultures is considered a form of flattery, whereas in many other cultures it is considered offensive and even illegal.

Thinking Critically

Have students read the information on **applying what you've learned** in the box on page 158. Elicit or give additional examples of when students could apply this critical thinking skill. For example: before reading an article about any new topic, students could take a few minutes to think about or list what they already know about the topic. Then they will be able to read more actively, thinking about why the author may or may not have included some information, or if the information is accurate. Then have students work in groups—of similar cultures, if possible— and discuss what they know about art in their own cultures.

Freewriting

5   Page 158.

By now students should be aware that the purpose of freewriting is to generate ideas on the page, and that they should not worry about grammar, spelling, or accuracy. Students should write freely about any art in the opening pages of this chapter or other pictures that may have been brought in to the classroom or that they might have seen in an art gallery. You might encourage them to describe the art first, especially if they are describing a work that they have viewed outside the classroom. Note that students will revise this freewriting later in Part 2 Activity 7 Student Book page 160.

Gathering Information

6   Page 158.

Have students choose an aspect of art first as a focus for their research, and then do research on the Internet or in the library. They can do this project individually, in pairs, or in small groups. Remind them to record bibliographic information about their sources as they take notes, and to bring in a photocopy or postcard of the art to incorporate into their presentation in Activity 7.

7   Page 158.

Encourage students to outline their presentation first, as if it were an essay, and to practice their presentation to be sure that it is five to ten minutes long. When students give their presentations, encourage the other students to take notes for use in a future writing assignment (Part 2, Activity 6, Student Book pg. 160).

Part 2 Language for Writing

Analyzing and Describing Art

Be sure that students understand the idea of specialized terms. Art has some specialized terms, which will be discussed in this section. Elicit other examples of fields with specialized terms, and some examples of specialized terms.

1   Page 159.

Have students work in groups to look at pictures and brainstorm what art words they already know. You can expand this activity further by having groups then merge and share their words. Explain that they can use these vocabulary words for their own writing and discussion activities in this chapter, and specifically in the subsequent writing activities 4–7 on page 160. If they are keeping a vocabulary log in this course, encourage them to add these words and to write them in sentences of their own.

2   Page 159.

Have students work individually or in pairs to locate the expressions about the functions of art in the article and discuss its meaning. You could also encourage them to write one additional example of their own for each of the following expressions.

3   Page 159.

Have students work in pairs to discuss what words they know in pairs and to guess the meanings of new words. Then have them check dictionary definitions and, if time permits, draw a picture to explain each word.

4   Page 160.

Have students describe the photos at the beginning of the chapter, using as many new words as they can. Then have students exchange descriptions and check for accurate word usage.

5   Page 160.

Have students write sentence individually and then exchange them in pairs to check for accuracy and clarity.

6 Page 160.

Encourage students to find a new work of art to describe and analyze, if possible. This assignment could work well in conjunction with a field trip to an art gallery or museum. One way that students could structure this writing is to write a paragraph of description followed by a paragraph of analysis of function and/or cultural values. Have students exchange paragraphs in pairs to check for clarity, organization, and vocabulary usage.

7 Page 160.

Have students return to their freewriting from Part 1 to formalize it and incorporate as many new words and expressions as possible. Then have students exchange paragraphs in pairs to check for clarity, organization, and vocabulary usage.

Part 3 Systems for Writing

Introductions

Introduce this topic by having a brief class discussion about strategies that students currently use or have used before when writing introductions, and what problems they sometimes find. Ask them to think about or even to find examples of introductions that draw them in and generate interest in the topic. The examples could come from previous chapters in this book, or from other sources. Then have students read the information in the boxes and the examples of different kinds of introductions. Students could read the examples individually, perhaps while you read them aloud, or they could take turns reading them aloud. Encourage them to discuss, as a class or in groups, which introductions they like best and why. If students have brought in sample introductions, they might look for the four strategies that are listed in the box: background information, quotations, definitions, or summaries.

1 Page 162.

Have students work individually to select an introduction from a previous essay, perhaps something from their writing portfolio, and rewrite it four different ways. Then have them exchange introductions (both the original and the revisions) with a partner. Encourage them to choose which of their partner's introductions they like best and to explain why they liked it.

Conclusions

Have a brief class discussion about conclusions: what strategies do they currently use, or have they used, for writing conclusions? What problems or frustrations do they sometimes encounter? If time permits, have students bring in examples of conclusions that they find effective or like. The examples could come from previous chapters in this book, or from other sources. Then have students read the information in the box. If they have brought in examples of conclusions that they like, have them discuss whether or not it includes features mentioned in the box, or additional features.

Focus on Testing

Having a Repertoire of Introductions and Conclusions

Have students read the information in the box. Encourage them to think about introduction and conclusion strategies when they plan their writing in a timed-essay situation. You might reinforce this concept when you assign one of the writing assignments on Student Book page 163.

2 Page 163.

Have students work individually to select a conclusion from a previous essay they wrote, perhaps something from their writing portfolio and rewrite it to include new information. Then have them exchange conclusions (both the original and the revision) with a partner. Encourage them to explain how their partner's conclusion improves upon the original.

Writing Assignments. Page 163.

Have students choose one of these topics for a writing assignment to complete at home or, alternatively, in class as a timed essay. If you give this as a homework assignment, encourage students to use their freewriting, discussion notes, and paragraphs they wrote from this chapter to help them with content. Have students write out a thesis statement, topic sentences, anticipated reader questions, possible supporting material, and an outline before beginning the assignment. Also encourage them to choose one of the four types of introductions. You may wish to have students turn in a detailed outline and a completed introduction before they do the actual writing, or have students check each other's outlines and introductions in pairs.

Part 4 Evaluating for Rewriting

Allow for plenty of class time for this process of drafting and revising. Students will be evaluating each other's drafts with particular criteria in mind for each stage of this process. Students can conduct peer reviews in a variety of ways, in pairs and small groups, orally and in writing; they may choose their own pairs or be assigned a partner by yourself. You may wish to vary the structure of peer review sessions throughout the course.

Evaluating the First Draft. Page 164.
Have students read the drafts silently and then discuss the general questions with their partner. They may find it useful to take notes on the questions to aid them in discussion.

Evaluating the Second Draft. Page 165.
Step 1 will work best if students write their answers, as they are looking for very specific things and, in question one, they are essentially writing an outline of their partner's essay. Students can show their answers to the author of the paper, or hold a discussion based on their answers. Students can keep the same partner from their peer review of the first draft, or work with a new partner.

Writing the Final Draft. Page 166.
If students are keeping a writing portfolio, have them add the final version of this essay. They can look back on it later to check their progress.

Video Activities: Women in Jazz

Before You Watch
Have students discuss the questions in small groups. To facilitate conversation and set a tone, you might consider bringing in some examples of jazz to play for students, by male and/or female artists.

Answer to 1: a. Billie Holiday

Watch
Play the video. Have students listen for the answers and write them. Play the video again, if necessary. Have students compare their answers in groups.

Answers: 1. c 2. b 3. a 4. a, c, d

Watch Again
Play the video. Have students listen for the answers and write them. Play the video again, if necessary. Have students compare their answers in groups.

Answers: 1. a. Ida Cox (woman) b. Netta May McKinney (woman) c. Maxine Sullivan (woman) d. Lester Young e. Cab Calloway f. Duke Ellington g. Count Basie h. Helen Humes (woman) 2. b 3. a 4. b

After You Watch
Help students to brainstorm and organize their ideas by allowing some prewriting time. First have them brainstorm or freewrite ideas about visual arts, looking back at the chapter or their notes if necessary. Then have them do the same for music. Next, have them circle the similarities on their lists and underline the differences. From this information, they should be able to write an opinion statement about whether or not the two media are mostly similar or different. Have them find supporting reasons for their opinion and write them in outline form. Encourage them to find specific examples and to anticipate reader questions. Once students have planned their essay, they could get together in pairs or groups, talk about their outlines, and get some preliminary feedback.

Conflict and Reconciliation

<table>
<tr>
<td valign="top">

Goals

- **Write about a conflict and a proposal for a reconciliation effort**
- **Use abstract nouns**
- **Recognize and use literal and stipulated definitions**
- **Interpret metaphors**
- **Brainstorm ideas in a test-taking situation**

</td>
<td valign="top">

Part 1 Ideas for Writing

Getting Started

1 Page 170.
Have students look at the pictures and captions, and have them complete the chart in small groups. You may need to point out in the examples in the chart that "vs" stands for "versus." This abbreviation (or sometimes simply "v.") is commonly used in legal cases or in statements about conflicting issues or people.

Sample Answers:

</td>
</tr>
</table>

Photo	What is the conflict?	Who is it between?	What is one solution?
1	Protection of animals and the environment vs. development	Environmentalists vs. people who support business, residential development	Limit development
2	Advancing medical and product research to benefit humans vs. saving animals	Scientific researchers vs. animal research protestors (organizations for the protection or ethical treatment of animals)	Try to find other ways of conducting research that do not harm animals; limiting animal research; having research groups adhere to strict guidelines
3	Spending more money on the military vs. spending money on other causes, like social issues	The government vs. lobbyists against military spending	Spend more money on social causes like education, crime prevention, welfare
4	Capital punishment vs. lifetime incarceration	Adocates of capital punishment vs. protestors against it	Have a group of political and religious leaders and scholars debate the implications of capital punishment and revise the policy in states that permit it.
5 (pg. 169)	Companies that manufacture products using chemicals (CFCs) that harm the ozone layer vs. using environmentally-friendly products and procedures	Environmental protestors vs. large companies	Have an organization help companies regulate and eventually cut down on their use of harmful products or procedures, and find environmentally-friendly alternatives.

Reading for Ideas

2 Prereading Questions. Page 171.

Have students discuss the prereading questions in groups, or have them write answers individually and then share them in groups. Answers will vary. For the words listed in number one, have students guess the meanings first, by thinking of the context or looking at word parts, and then have them check the meanings in the dictionary. Finally, have them read the article and the poem. They can read it silently, perhaps while you read it aloud, or they can take turns reading the paragraphs and the poem out loud.

3 Postreading Questions. Page 173.

Have students answer the questions individually, in pairs, or in groups. Encourage students to use their own words in their answers; they may find it easier to do so if they try to write their answers without looking back at the book. They could discuss the questions first in groups, looking up the information in the article, and paraphrase as a separate step.

Answers:

1. Snyder's constituency is the wilderness.
2. Sample paraphrase (answers will vary): "I would like to speak for an area that neither scholars nor government officials usually discuss."
3. Snyder discusses a conflict between the human and the nonhuman (people vs. nature).
4. Snyder advises us to learn about nature and tread lightly on the earth.
5. According to Snyder, one thing that is wrong with Western culture is that it alienates itself from the ground of its own being – the wilderness. (It is detached from nature, and therefore destroys it without conscience).
6. "Primitive" peoples can teach us about how to communicate with nature and respect it more.

Thinking Critically

Introduce the topic by writing eliciting or giving an example of a metaphor (a classic example, *My love is a rose.* Compare this with *My love is like a rose.* The former is a metaphor; the latter is a simile. Both types of figurative language make comparisons between two things; however, a metaphor does not use the word *like*). Have students read the information on **interpreting metaphors** in the box on page 174. Ask students what *hills* and *valleys* are being compared to (answers will vary; a possible answer is "endless problems"). To expand this activity and give students more practice with figurative language, you could ask them to list comparisons of their own (perhaps on the topic of nature/the environment) and write them as metaphors. They could also incorporate them into a short poem modeled after Snyder's.

Freewriting

4 Page 174.

Students could list possible conflicts first, and then choose one to freewrite about. When thinking of possible conflicts, you might encourage them to classify them into categories such as: *school, community, state, this country, another country, world.* In other words, they can think of conflict on a large scale or a relatively small scale. Note that students will use this information in Activity 5 Student Book page 175, and they will revise this freewriting later in Part 2 Activity 3 Student Book page 177.

Gathering Information

5 Page 175.

Have students circulate around the room and explain the conflict they freewrote about to each other. Students should take notes on six different conflicts, making sure that they have information to each of the three main questions. They may ask follow-up questions if they like. Set a time limit to be sure that everyone can continue to circulate and complete their charts.

6 Page 175.

Have students read the paragraph and work in groups to propose a solution. Remind them of the importance of reaching a consensus; a plan may have to be modified in order to incorporate everyone's ideas and feelings, or they may have to work harder to persuade group members of their point of view. Students can write up their proposal formally and present it to the class.

Part 2 Language for Writing

Using Abstract Nouns

Have students read the definition and examples of abstract nouns. Remind them that abstract nouns are used with singular verb forms, and that they cannot be pluralized because they are noncountable.

1 Page 176.

Have students work individually or in pairs to write definitions of eight words of their choice. Explain that they can use these vocabulary words for their own writing and discussion activities in this chapter, and specifically in the subsequent writing activities 3 and 4 Page 177. If they are keeping a vocabulary log in this course, encourage them to add these words.

2 Page 176.

Have students work individually or in pairs to incorporate five of the nouns into sentences related to a conflict. They could look back at the pictures in the beginning of the chapter for ideas, or write something related to their freewriting or to the chart of their classmates' information about conflicts (Part 1 Activity 5 Student Book page 175).

Giving Definitions

Have students read the expressions commonly used in defining words. Encourage them to add any additional expressions they may have come across.

3 Page 177.

Have students formalize their freewriting into a paragraph using abstract nouns. Encourage them to use phrases of definition if they find it necessary to define a word.

4 Page 177.

Have students summarize Snyder's argument in their own words, incorporating abstract nouns and definition phrases as much as possible. Then have students exchange finished paragraphs in pairs to check for accuracy and clarity.

Part 3 Systems for Writing

Definitions: Literal and Stipulated

Have students read the information in the boxes. Emphasize the fact that definitions can be useful in introductions and in the body paragraphs of the essay whenever it is appropriate to explain a word that the audience might be unfamiliar with, or that might have a special use. Have students read the examples of literal and stipulated definitions.

1 Page 178.

Have students work individually or in pairs to write literal (dictionary) definitions of the words and Snyder's stipulated definition (his interpretation of them).

Sample Answers:
1. seeds: literal = small parts of plants that will grow into new plants; stipulated (see line 17) = the beginnings of the end, the things that will cause its eventual destruction
2. teacher: literal = someone who instructs others, usually in a classroom situation; stipulated (see line 1): models, people who provide a good example for him and his beliefs
3. humanism: literal = a way of thinking that is concerned with human welfare and

values; stipulated (see line 6) = a way of thinking that includes consideration of – and representation of – the nonhuman (i.e., things from nature)

Focus on Testing

Brainstorming to Get Started

Have students read the information in the box. Remind them that they have probably already done brainstorming activities, individually or in groups, when they have listed ideas in preparation for a writing activity. Brainstorming usually involves quickly listing words or phrases; rarely does it involve complete sentences. It can involve word associations, word mapping, or idea-clustering. Encourage them to brainstorm ideas for a couple of minutes when they plan their writing in a timed-essay situation. You might reinforce this concept when you assign one of the writing assignments on Student Book page 179.

2 Page 179.

Have students work individually write a full paragraph about a conflict and possible resolution from one of the photographs at the beginning of the chapter. They may wish to refer to the chart they completed in Part 1 Activity 2. Encourage them to incorporate at least one definition of a specialized word; it can be literal or stipulated. Then have them exchange paragraphs with a partner to check for vocabulary usage and definitions.

3 Page 179.

Have students choose one of the words to write a stipulated definition. They should write how they would interpret the word in general, or they might think of a specific context and write a stipulated definition for that context. Have them exchange definitions with a partner to check for accuracy. Alternatively, you could add a game element to this activity by having students write definitions without saying the word; partners then have to use the definitions to guess each other's words. As another variation, to stress the contrast between a literal and a stipulated definition, you

could have students write both for the word that they choose (so that their definitions will look like those in Part 3 Activity 1).

4 Page 179.

Have students brainstorm first by listing possible subjects for the paragraph: people and the conflicts they were involved in. The person can be someone they know personally or somebody famous, like Martin Luther King, Jr.. Then have them choose the most interesting person and conflict from the list and write a paragraph. Encourage them to incorporate at least two definitions, one literal and one stipulated. Then have them exchange paragraphs with a partner to check for definitions and overall clarity. You could also have students underline or write down the literal and stipulated definitions in their partners' paragraphs.

Writing Assignments. Page 179.

Have students choose one of these topics for a writing assignment to complete at home or, alternatively, in class as a timed essay. If you give this as a homework assignment, encourage students to use their freewriting, discussion notes, and paragraphs they wrote from this chapter to help them with content. Have students write out a thesis statement, topic sentences, anticipated reader questions, possible supporting material, and an outline before beginning the assignment. Also encourage them to identify one or more words to define, and to write their stipulated definition in advance. You may wish to have students turn in a detailed outline and a stipulated definition before they do the actual writing, or have students check each other's outlines and definitions in pairs.

Part 4 Evaluating for Rewriting

Allow for plenty of class time for this process of drafting and revising. Students will be evaluating each other's drafts with particular criteria in mind for each stage of this process. Students can conduct peer reviews in a variety of ways, in pairs and small groups, orally and in writing; they may choose their own pairs or be assigned a partner by yourself. You may wish to vary the structure of peer review sessions throughout the course.

Evaluating the First Draft. Page 180.

Have students read the drafts silently and then discuss the general questions with their partner. They may find it useful to take notes on the questions to aid them in discussion.

Evaluating the Second Draft. Page 181.

Step 1 will work best if students write their answers, as they are looking for very specific things and, in question one, they are essentially writing an outline of their partner's essay. Students can show their answers to the author of the paper, or hold a discussion based on their answers. Students can keep the same partner from their peer review of the first draft, or work with a new partner.

Writing the Final Draft. Page 181.

If students are keeping a writing portfolio, have them add the final version of this essay. They can look back on it later to check their progress.

Video Activities: A Strike

Before You Watch

Have students discuss the questions in small groups.

Sample Answers: 1. Workers go on strike to put pressure on management in order to receive higher pay and better working conditions. 2. No

Watch [on video]

Play the video. Have students listen for the answers and write them. Play the video again, if necessary. Have students compare their answers in groups.

Answers: 1. b 2. b 3. b

Watch Again [on video]

Play the video. Have students listen for the answers and write them. Play the video again, if necessary. Have students compare their answers in groups.

Answers: 1. a, b, c, f, g 2. nurses 3. a, b 4. a 5. b 6. c

After You Watch

Help students to brainstorm and organize their ideas by allowing some prewriting time. First have them write freely about what they know and want to know about unions, or make a know/want to know chart. They may need to do some research on the Internet or in the library, or discuss and debate the pros and cons of unions with other students. Then have them list advantages and disadvantages and decide on an opinion. Have them outline the essay and write a thesis statement. Encourage them to find specific examples and to anticipate reader questions. Once students have planned their essay, they could get together in pairs or groups, talk about their outlines, and get some preliminary feedback.

Medicine and Science

Goals

- **Research and write about an aspect of medicine and healing**
- **Understand prefixes and suffixes in medical terminology**
- **Review transitions**
- **Make comparisons**
- **Use prediction as a critical thinking skill**
- **Get your thesis right in a test-taking situation**

Part 1 Ideas for Writing

Getting Started

1 Page 184.

Have students look at the pictures and captions and answer the questions individually. Then have them share their answers in small groups. Answers will vary.

2 Page 186.

Have students discuss the cultural aspects of medicine in small groups. One person from each group should record their ideas. Then have groups report their ideas and examples to the class.

Reading for Ideas

3 Prereading Questions. Page 187.

Have students discuss the prereading questions in groups, or have them write answers individually and then share them in groups. Answers will vary. Then have them read the article. They can read it silently, perhaps while you read it aloud, or they can take turns reading the paragraphs out loud.

4 Postreading Questions. Page 189.

Have students answer the questions individually, in pairs, or in groups. Encourage students to use their own words in their answers; they may find it easier to do so if they try to write their answers without looking back at the book. They could discuss the questions first in groups, looking up the information in the article, and paraphrase as a separate step.

Sample Answers:

1. The Americans are following a shaman, looking for medicinal cures in the Amazon rain forest. They are possibly "a little" uncomfortable because they are used to taking pills or conventional medicines for illnesses, and the shaman is asking them to taste ants!

2. Answers will vary.

3. The two "races" Royte describes are the race among companies to find plants before the rain forests are all destroyed, and the race among companies to profit from medicinal discoveries.

Thinking Critically

Have students read the information on **making predictions** in the box on page 189. Have them work in groups to make predictions about the rain forest and medicinal plants. Then ask them how they might apply prediction to other articles. Students can use prediction as a critical thinking skill by looking at the title, pictures, and subheadings of an article and predicting what kinds of information will or should be included. They can also think further about a topic by making future predictions.

Freewriting

5 Page 190.

Students can write freely about their opinion on the issue in general, or perhaps narrate an experience they have had and state their opinion at the end. Tell them that they can refer back to this freewriting activity later to help them with one of the writing assignments at the end of this chapter. Note that this freewriting activity will also be revised in Part 2 Activity 3 Student Book page 192.

Gathering Information

6 Page 190.

Students might return to their discussion notes from Part 1 Activities 1 and 2 for additional ideas of topics to research. Encourage students to use a combination of Internet /library research and interviewing, if possible. Remind students to keep bibliographic records of their sources.

7 Page 190.

Have students form small groups (different groups from those formed in Part 2, Activity 6); if possible, group them according to people who researched the same or very similar therapies. Have them read the "case studies" of people and their illnesses and describe treatment procedures for each. Then have them write up their treatments and share them with the class.

Part 2 Language for Writing

Understanding Prefixes and Suffixes in Medical Terminology

1 Page 191.

Remind students that prefixes and suffixes are parts of words whose meanings you can memorize to help you to define unknown words. Have students work in pairs to add to the chart with other medical words in various forms. They might look back at the article or at notes from their research for more ideas of words.

Answers: see chart below

Nouns	Nouns	Verbs	Adjectives	Adverbs
Medic	Medication	Medicate	Medicated	
	Medicine			Medicinally
Therapist	Therapy		Therapeutic	Therapeutically
Healer	Healing	Heal	Healing	
Herbalist	Herb		Herbal	
	Diagnosis	Diagnose	Diagnostic	
	Treatment	Treat	Treatable	
Practitioner	Practice	Practice		
Pharmacist	Pharmacy		Pharmaceutical	
Psychologist	Psychology	Psychoanalyze	Psychological	Psychologically
Biologist	Biology		Biological	Biologically

2 Page 192.

Have students work individually or in pairs to explain the words from the chart. Explain that they can use these vocabulary words for their own writing and discussion activities in this chapter, and specifically in the subsequent writing activities 3 and 4 Page 192). If they are keeping a vocabulary log in this course, encourage them to add these words.

Answers:

1. *Medicinal* is an adjective that relates to medicine. *Medical* is an adjective that relates to the study or practice of medicine.

2. A *diagnosis* is a health care practitioner's identification of a disease or injury. A *treatment* is a procedure of eliminating the symptoms and/or cause of the disease or injury.

3. a. a therapist b. an herbalist c. a pharmacist d. a psychologist e. a biologist . The ending (suffix) that these words have in common is *–ist*. Other fields in which the word for the practitioner has this ending: *dentist, artist, florist.*

4. The word *practice* has the same form as both and adjective and a noun.

3 Page 192.

Have students formalize their freewriting into a paragraph using as many medicine-related terms from the chart as possible. Then have students exchange finished paragraphs in pairs to check for clarity and for accurate word usage.

4 Page 192.

Have students write a paragraph of advice for each patient using as many new vocabulary words from the chart as possible. They can give advice from different medicinal approaches, or from one. Then have students exchange finished paragraphs in pairs to check for accuracy and clarity.

Reviewing Transitions

Introduce this topic by asking students to review what transitional expressions they have already learned and used. Have them give you examples; write them on the board. Ask students to tell you how they are used (i.e., to order information in a process, to show cause/effect, etc.). Tell students that transitions can be used within paragraphs (to show relationships of ideas between sentences) and between paragraphs (to show relationships of ideas between paragraphs and help the information flow smoothly); they can also be used as organizing principles for entire essays (comparison/contrast essays). Have students read the information above and in the chart. Point out that these transitions require different sentence patterns. Have students read the examples below the chart on page 193. For the third type of transition word/sentence pattern, linking independent clauses, you may wish to point out a punctuation alternative. Students can also use these words in one sentence, rather than using them to begin a new sentence, by placing a semicolon before the word and a comma after.

5 Page 193.

Students could either rewrite their paragraphs from Activity 4, incorporating transition words and sentence patterns, or write new paragraphs about two other patients. Have students exchange completed paragraphs in pairs and check for correct use of transition words.

6 Page 193.

Have students write their comparison of healing methods in one paragraph. If they are not sure how to organize it, assure them that organizational approaches will be discussed in the next session. For now, they should concentrate on using transition words correctly. Have students exchange completed paragraphs in pairs and check for correct use of transition words.

Part 3 Systems for Writing

Comparisons

Have students read the information in the boxes on page 194. Emphasize the fact that comparisons can be made at the paragraph-level or at the essay-level. Also highlight the importance of giving the reader a "road map" of the essay by using the thesis statement to indicate how the items will be compared (in other words, on what basis will the items be compared, and are the items primarily similar or different).

1 Page 194.

Have students work individually or in pairs to read the example thesis statements and answer the questions after Example B. The answers immediately follow the example, so you might encourage students to cover up the answers and try to analyze the statement on their own first.

2 Page 195.

Have students work individually or in pairs to predict and discuss the essay organization from example A. Have them read the two organizational patterns for examples A and B, and discuss possible advantages and disadvantages of this pattern. Note that one way to describe this simple compare/contrast organizational pattern is "block organization"; it involves discussing the first item in its entirety (in a "block"), and then the second. It does not tend to work well for more complicated or detailed topics, but works well for relatively straightforward comparisons.

3 Page 196.

Have students read example C and the more complex organizational pattern that follows. Have them discuss possible advantages and disadvantages of this pattern. Note that one way to describe this more complex organizational pattern is "point-by-point organization." The two items are compared in alternation, within each point of comparison. This approach works well for more complex topics, but is more challenging;

transition words should be used liberally so that the reader does not get lost.

Focus on Testing

Getting Your Thesis Right

Have students read the information in the box on page 197. Remind them that a good thesis provides a kind of "road map" to the essay, briefly mentioning points that will support the argument and that will be further developed in each paragraph. One way that they can "test" the thesis is to be sure that each body paragraph is about only one topic, and that the topic of the paragraph is briefly mentioned in the thesis. Students may find it useful to repeat key words from the thesis in the topic sentence of each paragraph. Encourage students to check their thesis against their topic sentences in a timed-essay situation. You might reinforce this concept when you assign one of the writing assignments on Student Book page 197.

4 Page 197.

Have students brainstorm for each item first, and then write possible thesis statements and outlines. Have them compare results with a partner and talk about their choices. Answers will vary.

Writing Assignments. Page 197.

Have students choose one of these topics for a writing assignment to complete at home or, alternatively, in class as a timed essay. If you give this as a homework assignment, encourage students to use their freewriting, discussion notes, and paragraphs they wrote from this chapter to help them with content. Have students write out a thesis statement, topic sentences, anticipated reader questions, possible supporting material, and an outline before beginning the assignment. Encourage them to try outlining their comparison/contrast essay both ways first. You may wish to have students turn in a detailed outline before they do the actual writing, or have students check each other's outlines in pairs.

Part 4 Evaluating for Rewriting

Allow for plenty of class time for this process of drafting and revising. Students will be evaluating each other's drafts with particular criteria in mind for each stage of this process. Students can conduct peer reviews in a variety of ways, in pairs and small groups, orally and in writing; they may choose their own pairs or be assigned a partner by yourself. You may wish to vary the structure of peer review sessions throughout the course.

Evaluating the First Draft. Page 198.

Have students read the drafts silently and then discuss the general questions with their partner. They may find it useful to take notes on the questions to aid them in discussion.

Evaluating the Second Draft. Page 199.

Step 1 will work best if students write their answers, as they are looking for very specific things and, in question one, they are essentially writing an outline of their partner's essay. Students can show their answers to the author of the paper, or hold a discussion based on their answers. Students can keep the same partner from their peer review of the first draft, or work with a new partner.

Writing the Final Draft. Page 200.

If students are keeping a writing portfolio, have them add the final version of this essay. They can look back on it later to check their progress.

Video Activities: Stealth Surgery

Before You Watch

Have students discuss the questions in small groups. Answers will vary.

Watch [on video]

Play the video. Have students listen for the answers and write them. Play the video again, if necessary. Have students compare their answers in groups.

Answers: 1. playing softball; it is unusual because he is 81 and just had surgery. 2. c 3. the Stealth system (or Stealth surgery) 4. It is less painful, less disfiguring, and requires less recovery time.

Watch Again [on video]

Play the video. Have students listen for the answers and write them. Play the video again, if necessary. Have students compare their answers in groups.

Answers: 1. MRI, CT scans, converted, images, placed, creates, anatomical 2. a 3. c 4. b 5. a 6. b

After You Watch

Help students to brainstorm and organize their ideas by allowing some prewriting time. First have debate the issue informally in small groups. Then have them write freely about what they know and want to know about the issue, or make a know/want to know chart. They may need to do some research on the Internet or in the library. Next have them list advantages and disadvantages of each position and decide on an opinion. Have them outline the essay with supporting reasons and write a thesis statement. Encourage them to find specific examples and to anticipate reader questions or opposing points of view.

The Future

Goals

- **Write about a prediction for the future**
- **Learn language for using computer technology and for making qualified predictions**
- **Learn summarizing strategies**
- **Write and edit your own evaluation questionnaire**
- **Learn considering alternative options as a critical thinking skill**

Part 1 Ideas for Writing

Getting Started

1   Page 204.

Have students look at the pictures and captions and answer the questions individually. Then have them share their opinions and examples in small groups. Have group members try to answer everyone's question for number 7.

2   Page 206.

Have students discuss one of the topics in small groups. One person from each group should record their ideas. Then have groups report their ideas to the class.

Reading for Ideas

3   Prereading Questions. Page 206.

Have students discuss the prereading questions in groups, or have them write answers individually and then share them in groups. Then have them read the interview answers. They can read them silently, perhaps while you read them aloud, or they can take turns reading the interview answers out loud.

4   Postreading Questions. Page 208.

Have students complete the chart individually, in pairs, or in groups. Encourage students to paraphrase the predictions into their own words. They should note that in some cases the prediction may apply to more than one field.

Answers to 1:

Prediction	Technology	Demographics (Human populations)	Human Relationships	Geriatrics
People will live twice as long as they live now.	X	X		X
Many people will have multiple-careers and periods of time dedicated to parenting or philanthropy	X		X	
The USA will have a new, multi-ethnic, multi-racial type of American		X		

Prediction	Technology	Demographics (Human populations)	Human Relationships	Geriatrics
Changes in health and technology will force us to face major moral dilemmas	X		X	X
The family unit will strengthen and the divorce rate will drop			X	
A black president will be elected		X	X	
Programs for the old will threaten the economy				X

Answers to 2 will vary.

Thinking Critically

Have students read the information on **considering alternative options** in the box on page 209. Remind them that they have already had some practice considering opposing points of view when they have debated an issue in groups, or when they have listed advantages and disadvantages about a topic. Have them work individually or in pairs to write opposing points of view for the issues listed. Encourage them to use this skill in their future writing by debating a topic with a partner or by writing down alternative options as they write.

Sample Answers: 1. Preserving jobs for loggers and clearing space for development need to be the priorities in this new century. 2. Cultural differences between people will become diminished or even erased as communication makes the world smaller. 3. Ending famine and poverty in developing countries is the single most important issue in our world. 4. The "information age" will bring people closer together by empowering them to communicate in new, efficient, and socially productive ways.

Freewriting

5 **Page 209.**
Students can write freely about their future predictions. Note that this freewriting activity will be revised in Part 2 Activity 4 Student Book page 212.

Gathering Information

6 **Page 210.**
Have students choose a topic to focus on and then do research in the library or on the Internet. Remind them to write down their sources and to take careful notes. The information will be used in a debate in Activity 7. They may wish to take more detailed notes on an additional piece of paper.

7 **Page 210.**
Have the class choose one topic to debate from the list. Have them suggest possible statements (or resolutions) about the topic. The resolutions must be debatable, not factual: people must be able to disagree about them. (You might tell them that this is also a good test for an effective thesis statement). Then have the class vote on the one that they would like to debate. Divide them into two teams. Allow plenty of time for them to prepare their arguments and examples. Remind them of the format for a formal debate; they have already done this in Chapter 8, Student Book pg.

142. Remind groups to assign everyone a role so that everyone participates equally.

Using Computer Terminology

1 Page 211.

This activity presents a game element to learning computer-related vocabulary. Remind students that they can use these vocabulary words for their own writing and discussion activities in this chapter, and specifically in the subsequent writing activities 2 through 5 on page 212. If they are keeping a vocabulary log in this course, encourage them to add these words.

Making Qualified Predictions

Introduce the topic by eliciting some examples from students. Ask them to give you some predictions about which they are certain. Write these sentences on the board with *will*. For example: We *will* continue to pay taxes next year. Then ask for predictions about which they are less certain—things that are possible. Write these sentences on the board with *could*. For example: We *could* face a recession next year. Explain that modals can be used to express certainty and possibility with predictions. Have students read the information on page 211 and the example of an understood conditional (a conditional in which the if clause is understood but not written). Elicit additional examples of future predictions with understood conditionals.

2 Page 212.

Have students work individually to make predictions about themselves in the future; you might even put a timeline on the board to give students specific dates to work with. Have students share their answers with the class or in pairs and check for correct sentence structure with modals.

3 Page 212.

Elicit a definition of a futurist. Students should recognize the suffix –ist from the previous chapter, and know that a futurist is a kind of practitioner: here, someone who makes predictions about the future. Have students read the instructions and the paragraph. Students can work individually or in pairs to rewrite the paragraph to express less certainty.

Answer:

The world of work is changing, fundamentally and decisively, according to futurist Daniel Bell, professor of social sciences at Harvard University.

In the new society, "work <u>could be</u> a game between people," according to Bell. This contrasts with the nature of work in the factory-centered industrial society, which he called "a game against manufactured nature and the machine," and that of preindustrial work such as agriculture, "a game against nature."

"[The] nine-to-five [work day] <u>could be</u> obsolete," he says. "Work hours <u>could be</u> staggered, individualized; more facilities <u>could be</u> used twenty-four hours a day. The computer revolution <u>could enable</u> people to conduct their business at home, at the beach, wherever they choose."

4 Page 212.

Have students formalize their freewriting into a paragraph, using modals to express degrees of certainty. Then have students exchange finished paragraphs in pairs to check for clarity and correct use of modals.

5 Page 212.

You may wish to give students some time to brainstorm ideas first. Tell them that by *community* they can think of any community, large or small: school, neighborhood, religious, workplace, etc. Encourage them to use as many computer-related words as they can, and to use modals to express degrees of certainty. Have students exchange completed paragraphs in pairs and check for correct usage and overall clarity

Part 3 Systems for Writing

Summarizing

Have students read the information in the boxes on page 212 and 213. Emphasize the fact that a summary must be considerably shorter than the original. A summary of a paragraph might be one or two sentences long. A summary of an essay might be one or two paragraphs long. A summary of a book might be one or two pages long, at the most. Summaries are shorter because not all details are included. Also point out that students must change the words and sentence structures from the original as much as possible—they must explain the ideas "in their own words" (except for specialized terminology). A good way to do this is to read the text carefully, and then write the summary without looking back at it, thus avoiding the temptation to borrow heavily from the author's own words.

1 Page 213.

Have students work individually or in pairs to read and analyze the example summary.

Sample Answers:

1. The original article is one page long. The summary is one paragraph (two sentences).

2. The purpose of the first sentence in the summary is to give the name of the article and to state generally what it is about.

3. There are six main ideas in the original article. The same ideas are discussed in the summary.

4. The order of ideas in the summary is the same as in the original article.

5. These details do not appear in the summary. They are considered minor points that are used to illustrate the main points, and are therefore not necessary in a summary.

6. The ideas expressed in the summary are those that appear the original article. We know this because the title of the article is given immediately, and the author of the summary does not indicate his or her own opinion.

7. In the original article, future tenses are used because predictions are being made. In the summary, the present tense is used to introduce the article and the main ideas; future tenses are used only to indicate the future predictions from the original article.

Focus on Testing

Mastering the Art of Summary Writing

Have students read the information in the box. Encourage them to practice writing a summary of every article that they read, and to always check it for the criteria listed in the box on page 213. Have them also work on writing summaries more quickly, perhaps setting increasingly shorter time limits. You might reinforce this concept when you assign one of the writing assignments on Student Book page 215, or when students practice summarizing articles in Activity 2 Student Book page 215.

2 Page 215.

If you want to help students summarize more quickly, to simulate a test-taking situation, you could set them time limits for each summary, working towards less time by the final topics. Or students could write the summaries individually on their own time. Have them compare and evaluate summaries with a partner.

Writing Assignments. Page 215.

Have students choose one of these topics for a writing assignment to complete at home or, alternatively, in class as a timed essay. If you give this as a homework assignment, encourage students to use their freewriting, discussion notes, and paragraphs they wrote from this chapter to help them with content. Have students write out a thesis statement, topic sentences, anticipated reader questions, possible supporting material, and an outline before beginning the assignment. Encourage them to try outlining their comparison/contrast essay both ways first. You may wish to have students turn in a detailed outline before they do the actual writing, or have students check each other's outlines in pairs.

Part 4 Evaluating for Rewriting

Allow for plenty of class time for this process of drafting and revising. Students will be evaluating each other's drafts with particular criteria in mind for each stage of this process. Students can conduct peer reviews in a variety of ways, in pairs and small groups, orally and in writing; they may choose their own pairs or be assigned a partner by yourself. You may wish to vary the structure of peer review sessions throughout the course.

Evaluating the First Draft. Page 215.

Have students read the drafts silently and then discuss the general questions with their partner. They may find it useful to take notes on the questions to aid them in discussion.

Evaluating the Second Draft. Page 216.

By now, students should have become familiar with the types of questions asked in evaluating a second draft. Have students work in pairs to review the writing points presented throughout the book and devise their own questionnaire. Limit them to ten questions, partly in order to use time efficiently, and partly to force them to prioritize writing objectives. Then have then conduct their last peer review with the questionnaires they have devised. You may wish to collect everyone's questionnaire and copy them (or the best ones) for all class members to use as checklists for writing assignments in the future, or simply for comparison.

Writing the Final Draft. Page 216.

If students are keeping a writing portfolio, have them add the final version of this essay. Consider assigning a self-evaluation activity, in which students look at their progress throughout all the assignments and assess their own progress, perhaps in the form of a letter to you.

Video Activities: Concept Cars

Before You Watch

Have students discuss the questions in small groups. Encourage them to draw a picture or diagram of their ideal car in question 2.

Answers: 1. b 2. Answers will vary.

Watch [on video]

Play the video. Have students listen for the answers and write them. Play the video again, if necessary. Have students compare their answers in groups.

Answers: 1. b 2. b 3. a. the Lacrosse b. the Prowler c. the Avalanche

Watch Again [on video]

Play the video. Have students listen for the answers and write them. Play the video again, if necessary. Have students compare their answers in groups.

Answers: 1. a, c, d, f 2. a 3. b 4. c

After You Watch

Help students to brainstorm and organize their ideas by allowing some prewriting time. Have them write freely about what features are important to them in a car (safety? Attractiveness? Comfort? Speed? Performance?) Students may find it useful to draw the car. You could also bring in or have them bring in pictures of cars from magazines so that they have some more car-related vocabulary to work with. Then have them describe their ideal car and incorporate their reasons for wanting these features. They could write this description in a straightforward way, or they could write it as an advertisement for a car to be developed complete with a name, model number, and price. Encourage them to be creative and to have fun!

Writing Placement Test

Part 1 Knowledge about Writing

Please indicate whether each of the following statements is true or false.

Example:

__F__ **Question marks are never put at the end of a sentence containing a question.**

___ 1   Good writers remember to indent the first word of a paragraph.

___ 2. A comma can be placed at the end of a sentence.

___ 3. Commas can be used to separate items in a list.

___ 4. Be certain that you do not leave any space between the period and the first word of the next sentence.

___ 5. Don't capitalize small words like *a, the, to with* and *at* except at the beginning of a sentence.

___ 6. Don't capitalize the names of languages such as the language spoken in China.

___ 7. Use a comma after *yes* or *no* in an answer. For example: *Yes, I like flowers.*

___ 8. Always capitalize school subjects such as Algebra and Chemistry.

___ 9. Do not use quotation marks with exact quotes.

___10. Use an apostrophe to make possessive nouns.

___11. A topic sentence is frequently the last sentence of a paragraph.

___12. One thing that writers do not need to worry about is transitions from paragraph to paragraph.

___13. Supporting sentences should be relevant to the theme of the paragraph.

___14. A written summary is always longer than the original work.

___15. If you are writing an essay for an academic class you will want to have a conclusion.

Part 2 Sentence Completion

Select the best word, words or phrase to complete each sentence. Be sure to look at the contents of each sentence.

Example:

I want the pretty necklace _____.

   (a.) that is on sale

   b. who is on sale

   c. what is on sale

   d. where it is on sale

1. The restaurant has excellent food, _____.

   a. so I never eat there

   b. so I always eat there

   c. I never eat there

   d. I always eat there

2. I want to go to Mexico, _____.

   a. but I have lots of money

   b. but I don't speak Spanish fluently

   c. so I speak Spanish fluently

   d. I speak Spanish fluently

3. There's a movie theater _____ the left hand side of the street.

   a. at

   b. in

   c. on

   d. off

4. Louise screamed, _____

   a. There's a fire upstairs.

   b. "There's a fire upstairs."

   c. "That there is a fire upstairs."

   d. There's "a fire upstairs."

5. **She ate lunch _____.**

   a. as soon she finished writing the report

   b. when the report ends

   c. while the report ends

   d. as soon as the meeting ended

6. **The teacher_____ tells jokes in class, is very popular.**

   a. what

   b. who

   c. that

   d. there

7. **Another easy-to-prepare dish is quiche, _____.**

   a. what is wonderful for lunch

   b. is brunch

   c. is wonderful for brunch

   d. which is wonderful for brunch

8. **_____ I broke my leg, I have had a great deal of difficulty trying to get around.**

   a. When

   b. Which

   c. Since

   d. What

9. **She drinks a lot of plain water _____.**

   a. because she desperately wants to gain weight

   b. because she desperately wants to lose weight

   c. but she desperately wants to lose weight

   d. when she desperately wants to gain weight

10. **I have been an avid reader since _____.**

    a. I have walked a lot

    b. I have been young

    c. I was a young child

    d. I am walking

11. I can't go out for dinner tonight _____.

    a. because storms often come

    b. because of a storm that is due in at about eight o'clock

    c. because I love to go out for dinner

    d. because there will be a storm tomorrow at dinner time

12. If I were in love, _____.

    a. I would get married

    b. I got married

    c. I am getting married

    d. I get married next week

13. _____ the steamed fish nor the fried chicken are terribly spicy.

    a. Either

    b. Nor

    c. Neither

    d. Or

14. She said that _____

    a. "wanted something to eat."

    b. wanted something to eat.

    c. she wanted something to eat.

    d. "she wanted something to eat."

15. Deceit _____ mistrust.

    a. can causes

    b. results

    c. causes of

    d. can cause

Part 3 Organization

Read the following sentences. Please select the best sentence to follow the sentence given.

Example:

This morning we ate the most wonderful waffles, brimming with blueberries, for breakfast.

 a. I like meat and potatoes.

 b. I eat blueberries every night.

 (c.) My husband made some wonderful French roast coffee to go with the waffles.

 d. I don't like coffee.

1. **Children often have trouble getting up in the morning to go to school.**

 a. For example, children love to get up in the morning.

 b. This probably wouldn't happen if they did not stay up as late at night.

 c. Once children get to school they can take naps.

 d. Children always like going to school and are anxious to be punctual.

2. **The Mexican government wishes to curtail pollution in Mexico City.**

 a. They will try a number of different approaches to increase this problem.

 b. I don't worry about pollution very much.

 c. The people who are north of the Mexican border think that their own pollution is severe.

 d. A wide variety of strategies impacting everyone from motorists to industrial polluters have been introduced.

3. **It is very simple to make microwave popcorn.**

 a. Popcorn always gets stuck between my teeth.

 b. I don't know how much popcorn costs.

 c. I buy popcorn when I go to the movies.

 d. All you have to do is know how to push the buttons on the outside of the microwave oven.

4. **I firmly believe that children under the age of 21 should be prohibited from smoking.**

 a. I think that smoking is something that young people enjoy doing.

 b. I really don't really have any strong convictions one way or the other about teenage smoking.

 c. I was very poor and could not afford to do anything not even buy cigarettes for my mother.

 d. My heart aches when I see a teenager light up a cigarette.

5. Thank you so much for the gorgeous necklace.

   a. You should have bought something that was a little more expensive.

   b. Necklaces always look better on women who are much younger than I am.

   c. I have worn it several times and always receive compliments.

   d. Next time can we please go shopping for necklaces together?

Part 4 Writing

Your teacher will tell you if you should write a paragraph or an essay.

Write a Paragraph

Please select one of the following topics listed below and write a paragraph. Feel free to make some notes on a separate sheet of paper before you start writing.

1. Think of all of the different foods that you like to eat when you are at home. Please write about a food that you would serve to your guests.

2. Think about the different places that people go to on vacation. Please write about the location where you would like to go for your vacation.

3. Think about your favorite time of day. You might want to consider whether or not you are a morning or night person. Please write about your favorite time of day.

Write an Essay

Please select one of the topics listed below. Write an essay about your selection.

1. Think about the different academic subjects that one can study in school. Think about one that you really liked and one that you did not like as well. Please write a subject that you liked and compare it with one that you did not like as well. Be sure to comment on aspects such as the level of difficulty, the quality of instruction, etc. etc.

2. Think about different people who have helped you over time and made a difference in your life. Please write about how they helped you and what your life might have been like if they had not been part of it.

3. Think about the different modes of transportation such as walking versus taking the subway. Please write about a mode of transportation that is quick and compare it to one that is very slow. Be sure to comment on the advantages and disadvantages of each.

Name _____ **Date** _____

1. Match each word with its definition. (5 points)

___	1. proficient	a.	conversation between two people
___	2. multilingual	b.	the language you want to learn
___	3. criteria	c.	purpose
___	4. total immersion	d.	very good at something
___	5. dialogue	e.	a course used for real situations
___	6. nonnative speaker	f.	only the target language spoken in class
___	7. motive	g.	able to speak more than one language
___	8. a practical program	h.	speaks a language as a first language
___	9. target language	i.	values used to make a judgment
___	10. native speaker	j.	doesn't speak target language as a first language

2. Number the sentences in order. (5 points)

_____ On the other hand, people who are multilingual sometimes feel that although they know several languages, they may not feel one hundred percent comfortable with any of them.

_____ One advantage, of course, is that if you can understand and speak more than one language, you can understand and talk to more people from different cultures.

_____ There are both advantages and disadvantages to being multilingual.

_____ They may feel as though they are "linguistic nomads," traveling from one language to another but never using one long enough to feel at home with it.

_____ Many people feel that you can understand a culture better when you know the language.

3. Circle the letter of the correct answer. (5 points)

1. Which of these sentences is incorrect?

   a. My friend Sonia didn't have a strong motive for studying English; therefore, she did not progress very rapidly.

   b. My friend Sonia didn't have a strong motive for studying English; otherwise, she did not progress very rapidly.

   c. My friend Sonia didn't have a strong motive for studying English; however, she progressed very rapidly.

2. Which of these sentences is correct?

   a. Effective foreign language teachers shouldn't spend too much class time talking; thus, they should allow time for students to practice speaking.

   b. Effective foreign language teachers shouldn't spend too much class time talking; on the contrary, they should allow time for students to practice speaking.

   c. Effective foreign language teachers shouldn't spend too much class time talking; whereas, they should allow time for students to practice speaking.

3. Which of these sentences is incorrect?

   a. You should list all of your criteria when you research language programs.

   b. You should list all of the qualities you are looking for when you research language programs.

   c. You should list all of your criterion when you research language programs.

4. Which of these sentences is correct?

   a. There are three things you should consider when signing up for a language course: your motives, the school's methods, and the teacher's philosophy and background.

   b. There are three things you should consider when signing up for a language course: your motives, what are the school's methods, and researching the philosophy and background of the teacher.

   c. There are three things you should consider when signing up for a language course: motives, methods, and to learn the teacher's philosophy and background.

5. Which of these sentences is correct?

   a. Will you need to learn English for traveling phrases or for real proficient?

   b. Will you need to learn English for traveling phrases or for really proficient?

   c. Will you need to learn English for traveling phrases or for real proficiency?

4. Read this text and then answer the following questions. (5 points)

Many students learn English with the goal of eventually studying at a college or university in the United States; however, for these students, it may not be enough to gain proficiency in speaking, listening, reading, and writing the language. They may also benefit from taking classes in English for Academic Purposes (EAP). These types of classes cover areas specific to academic situations. For example, they might give students practice listening to lectures and taking notes. Professors may talk very quickly in a lecture, and students need a lot of practice listening for main ideas. In addition, classes in EAP might train students to write in the American academic style, which can be very different from the academic writing style in other countries. Specifically, American academic essays prove a thesis statement that stated early in the essay. In other countries, academic essays may present different ideas about a topic and lead up to a conclusion or opinion at the end. Finally, EAP classes can cover areas of concern to students' day-to-day lives, such as how to talk to a professor, what a professor's "office hours" are, how to participate in class discussions, and what basic classroom procedures are like. For these reasons, an EAP class is probably a useful supplement to a basic language program for anyone thinking of studying in another country.

1. What is the writer's purpose in this paragraph?

   a. to entertain the reader

   b. to persuade the reader to study in the United States

   c. to explain several advantages of taking an EAP course

2. Which sentence best summarizes the paragraph?

   a. A course in English for Academic Purposes may be a
   useful supplement to an English language course, since
   the American academic system can be very different from that of other countries.

   b. A course in general English proficiency is inferior to a course in English for Academic Purposes.

   c. A course in EAP should be required for anyone considering studying at an American university.

3. Which of these areas would probably not be covered in an EAP class?

   a. How to talk to a professor

   b. How to order food in a restaurant

   c. How to listen for main ideas and take notes in a lecture

4. In what way might the American academic essay format be different from academic essays in other countries?

   a. The American academic essay consists entirely of opinions and no facts.

   b. The American academic essay explores several different ideas first and then lead up to a thesis statement at the end of the essay.

   c. The American academic essay states a thesis statement in the beginning and then systematically proves and supports it.

5. How many supporting reasons does the writer give in this paragraph to support the topic sentence?

  a. six

  b. three

  c. one

5. Complete the following sentences (5 points)

1. In a paragraph, you develop and support _____.

  a. at least one main idea

  b. only one main idea

  c. several ideas

2. In an essay, you develop and support _____.

  a. a topic sentence

  b. an introduction

  c. a thesis

3. *On the contrary, however,* and *therefore* are examples of _____.

  a. coordinating conjunctions

  b. transition words and phrases

  c. adjectives

4. The thesis of an academic essay usually communicates _____ about an issue.

  a. an opinion

  b. a fact

  c. a topic

5. One purpose of an academic essay is to give information to _____.

  a. express the writer's thoughts in a personal and creative manner

  b. state and restate one idea in a variety of ways

  c. logically support or prove an opinion

Chapter 2 Quiz

Name _____   **Date** _____

1. Match each word with its definition. (5 points)

___ 1. forbidden   a. competitor

___ 2. legendary   b. distant

___ 3. expedition   c. a way to hide one's identity

___ 4. ardent   d. not permitted

___ 5. endeavor   e. strong-willed

___ 6. rival   f. attempt

___ 7. ascend   g. a journey to explore

___ 8. pioneer   h. climb to the top

___ 9. disguise   i. famous

___ 10. remote   j. one of the first people to do something

2. Number the sentences in order. (5 points)

___ In sum, these three examples suggest that having a superior education or specialized academic background is not necessarily the most important thing.

___ Courage is also important, for explorers can suddenly find themselves in relative isolation and in extremely difficult or dangerous situations.

___ Explorers tend to exhibit three main qualities: a spirit of adventure, courage, and self-discipline.

___ Another important quality is self-discipline, since explorers must fight the inevitable urge to quit when things become overwhelming or difficult.

___ One important quality is the desire to venture across new frontiers – to go where no one has gone before in terms of distance or knowledge.

3. Circle the letter of the correct answer. (5 points)

1. Which of these sentences is a good thesis statement?
   a. Mountain-climbers are usually prepared for their expeditions, but there are two areas that they may neglect to prepare for: the psychological states of isolation and of fear.
   b. Most people would agree that mountain-climbers are usually prepared for their expeditions.
   c. Mountain-climbers are usually prepared for their expeditions, but there are two areas that they may neglect to prepare for: the psychological states of isolation and of loneliness.

2. Here is an example thesis statement for an essay: "There are many adventure shows on television these days, but none of them give an accurate picture of the real hardships and success that true adventurers experience." What is the *topic* of this statement?

   a. None of them give an accurate picture of the real hardships and successes.

   b. There are many adventure shows on TV these days.

   c. The hardships and successes that real adventurers experience.

3. Here is an example of a thesis statement for an essay: "Many nineteenth-century explorers and the Indian guide Sacagawea helped to chart territory and give rise to maps that we continue to use today." What is wrong with the supporting ideas?

   a. They are not distinct.

   b. They are not balanced.

   c. They do not have the same level of generality.

4. Here is an example of a thesis statement for an essay: "Many intellectual frontiers have been crossed in the last decade, with the most important explorations occurring in the areas of genetic research and computer technology." How will the author develop the essay?

   a. Discuss developments first in genetic research and then in computer technology.

   b. Discuss developments in intellectual frontiers in the last decade, then developments in genetic research, and finally developments in computer technology.

   c. Discuss developments in computer technology and the in genetic research.

5. Here is an example of a thesis statement for an essay: "The government should fund embryonic stem-cell research." What is wrong with it?

   a. Its supporting ideas are not balanced.

   b. It does not state the writer's opinion or attitude about the topic.

   c. It does not introduce supporting ideas or predict the development of the essay.

4. Read this text and then answer the following questions. (5 points)

There are many new "reality" adventure shows on TV these days that glamorize danger and daring in the wilderness. Despite the wide appeal of these shows, they fail in several important areas. First of all, they fail to present an accurate picture of what it is really like to survive in the wilderness. Anyone who has been stranded somewhere outdoors for any length of time, or who has gotten lost on a hiking trip, will understand the real fear and isolation that sets in. The contestants on these shows, however, are surrounded by TV cameramen and producers all day. They know they are not in real danger, and the presence of TV crews serves as a constant reminder that they are in no way cut off from civilization. Moreover, these shows fail to educate people about the regions that the shows are set in. It is irresponsible to talk about people on a TV show who are "starving" and "suffering" when in fact indigenous peoples in these regions have been struggling to find food and survive harsh climates for years. Viewers come away from watching these shows with a greater knowledge about the psychology, hobbies, and romantic interests of the contestants, but with virtually no knowledge of the history and culture of the regions where the shows. Many viewers cannot even find the location of the shows on a map! Finally, the real failure of these shows is that they bring out the worst in our society. By emphasizing competition among mean-spirited individuals, rather than cooperation among team members working for a common cause, they paint an extremely negative picture of how our society operates and what values it holds. Such a picture suggests that this attitude of "survival of the fittest" is something to strive for in our everyday lives. It is unlikely that producers will stop making these shows in the near future, because they are so profitable. It is my hope, then, that viewers will watch them with a more critical eye—or, better yet, stop watching them altogether before these shows cause further harm to our society.

1. How does the writer feel about the trend of wilderness adventure shows on TV?

    a. amused

    b. angry

    c. indifferent

2. Which sentence best summarizes the writer's opinion?

    a. TV producers should stop making adventure "reality" shows immediately.

    b. People should realize that "reality" shows really do reflect the worst of our society.

    c. The new adventure "reality" shows on TV fail in three areas and thus may negatively impact our society.

3. What is the best way to express the supporting points the writer gives to support his or her opinion?

    a. The "reality" shows are inaccurate, uneducational, and psychologically harmful.

    b. The "reality" shows show people surrounded by camera crews, don't show native peoples gathering food and surviving harsh climates, and show mean-spirited people competing with each other.

    c. The "reality" shows are inaccurate, misleading, uneducational, irresponsible, mean-spirited, and harmful to society.

4. What is one example the writer gives to support the idea that these shows are uneducational?

    a. The shows do not depict all people on the camera crew that are actually there.

    b. People should cooperate as teams, not compete as individuals.

    c. Many viewers cannot even find the location of the shows on a map.

5. Which sentence best expresses what the writer most like his or her readers to do as a result of reading this article?

    a. Criticize the producers of these shows.

    b. Think critically about what they are watching, if they are going to continue watching these shows.

    c. Urge people in society to stop watching these shows.

5. Complete the following sentences (5 points)

1. A good thesis statement must have _____.

    a. a fact that most people can accept without disagreement

    b. a topic and an angle

    c. at least three supporting ideas

2. The purpose of an *angle* is to present _____.

    a. the general subject of the essay

    b. the thesis statement for the essay

    c. the writer's opinion about the topic and the approach to developing the essay

3. Supporting ideas should have the same _____.

    a. opinion of the writer

    b. degree of generality or specificity

    c. way of using facts as specific examples

4. If supporting ideas are not distinct, they are _____.

    a. too similar to develop into separate paragraphs in the essay

    b. not similar enough to support the thesis statement

    c. not important enough to be used to support the thesis statement

5. If one supporting idea is about someone's personal achievement, and another idea is about an achievement that benefits science in general, we would probably say that the supporting ideas do not have _____.

    a. the same degree of generality or specificity

    b. enough distinction

    c. he same degree of importance

Name _____   **Date** _____

1. Match each word with its definition. (5 points)

___   1. empathy   a. freeing

___   2. intimacy   b. with confidence

___   3. assertive   c. differing

___   4. findings   d. mutual understanding

___   5. anonymous   e. control

___   6. liberating   f. feeling what another person feels

___   7. rapport   g. closeness

___   8. varying   h. communicate with another person

___   9. relate   i. results of research

___ 10. dominate   j. unknown identity

2. Number the sentences in order. (5 points)

___ Women, on the other hand, tend to cross their legs, fold their hands in their lap, and sit or stand far from the person with whom they are speaking.

___ Another term for the "body language" that researchers have observed is nonverbal communication; it is the way in which people communicate through gestures and facial expressions.

___ The next time you observe men and women speaking, look for these examples of body language that have been described and ask yourself: do men's actions speak louder than women's?

___ Some of the researchers have found that men tend to take up more physical space, sit with their legs slightly apart, and lean in toward the person with whom they are speaking.

___ Some researchers, following the saying "actions speak louder than words," have observed the body language of men and women as they speak.

3. Circle the letter of the correct answer. (5 points)

1. Which of these sentences is correct?

    a. Some people see the Web as a place where gender does not matter, whereas others see it as a place where gender matters greatly.

    b. Some people see the Web as a place where gender does not matter whereas however others see it as a place where gender matters greatly.

    c. Whereas some people see the Web as a place where gender does not matter, on the other hand others see it as a place where gender matters greatly.

2. Which of these sentences is correct?

   a. A few years ago the Web was male-dominated, however today it is used almost equally by men and women.

   b. While a few years ago the Web was male-dominated, however today it is used almost equally by men and women.

   c. A few years ago the Web was male-dominated; however, today it is used almost equally by men and women.

3. Here is an example of a sentence used in a paragraph: "If parents truly want to challenge traditional gender roles in our society, they should begin by not giving their children gender-specific toys to play with." Which of the questions below is the best reader question to anticipate?

   a. Who should be challenging traditional gender roles?

   b. What are some examples of gender-specific toys?

   c. What is one way to challenge traditional gender roles?

4. Which example is the best to use to support a main idea in an academic essay analyzing the relationship between communication and gender?

   a. Somebody once said that men and women seem to be from different planets; this could explain why they have so many communication problems.

   b. According to Mary Smith, who wrote to an online message board for the Oprah Winfrey show, men and women probably don't communicate in the same way; she thinks this may be why she and her husband have so many problems.

   c. According to Deborah Tannen, author of the acclaimed bestseller *You Just Don't Understand,* men and women communicate so differently that they really speak different languages.

5. Here is an example of a sentence used in a paragraph: "Efforts toward women's rights have come a long way, but women still statistically earn less money than men." Think about possible reader questions. Which of these sentences would be the best choice to write immediately after the sentence you just read?

   a. Many women struggle to balance the demands of work and family.

   b. More and more women are choosing to delay marriage and childbirth well into their thirties in order to focus on their careers.

   c. According to a recent study by researchers at Blaine University, a woman in a middle-management position earns, on average, two-thirds of what a man earns in an equivalent position.

4. Read this text and then answer the following questions. (5 points)

Alex Mitchell, 39, pushes daughter, Dawn, 3, on a swing at a playground near their home. Dawn's twin sister, Melissa, plays in a sandbox with some other children a few yards away. Alex watches and plays with both children, just like any of the other parents that have accompanied their children to the park on this day. Except for one thing: Alex is the only father on the playground. Everyone else is a mother.

Alex is a stay-at-home father, and part of a growing trend of changes in the family dynamic in the United States. He used to be a stockbroker on Wall Street. His wife, Jan, has a successful career with an advertising agency. "Although we had the money, we knew that we didn't want to put our children in daycare to be raised by strangers," Alex explains. "When it came time to choose who should stay home with them, I was the best candidate. I was burned out from all the stress at work, and was no longer really enjoying my job. Jan loves her job, and had a limited time for maternity leave. Jan makes enough money to support the family, and is happy to do so, and I was happy to stay home with the children and run the household."

Alex's work is by no means easy. His day begins at 6:00, or sometimes earlier, when the children awaken. He makes breakfast for the family before Jana leaves for work. He cleans the house, does laundry, shops for groceries, all the while keeping a close eye on the twins, who are full of energy. In the afternoon, he starts making dinner, so that when Jan comes home they can all eat together. It's a long day, every day. "But I wouldn't trade this time at home with my children for anything," says Alex with a smile, as Dawn laughs with joy on the swing. "This is the best job in the world."

1. What word best describes the type of text this is?

   a. A human interest newspaper or magazine article

   b. A formal academic essay

   c. A research report

2. Which sentence best summarizes the writer's opinion?

   a. There is an increasing trend of stay-at-home fathers in the U.S.

   b. More fathers should choose to stay at home with their children.

   c. The writer does not directly give an opinion.

3. Of these possible reasons for an increasing number of stay-at-home fathers in the U.S., which can be inferred from the article?

   a. Women typically earn more money than men these days.

   b. Working in the home and raising children is less stressful than working in an office.

   c. Men are finding satisfaction in spending quality time with their children.

4. Which of these sentences is a good thesis statement for an academic essay about this text?

   a. The writer talks about Alex Mitchell, who is a stay-at-home father.

   b. The personal stories of men like Alex Mitchell suggest that being a stay-at-home father has at least three benefits that men would find attractive.

   c. his article proves that being a stay-at-home father is an increasing trend.

5. How might the writer rewrite this text to be an academic essay?

   a. Add more quotations and examples from experts on family life.

   b. State an opinion about stay-at-home fathers and prove it with two or three supporting points.

   c. Include more stories about or testimonies from stay-at-home fathers.

5. Complete the following sentences (5 points)

1. The body paragraphs of an essay typically _____.

   a. give the thesis statement

   b. anticipate and answer readers' possible questions

   c. state and restate the writer's opinion from the thesis statement

2. Body paragraphs of an essay also commonly _____.

   a. include very long quotations with little or no analysis

   b. include charts and graphs

   c. include specific facts and examples to illustrate the writer's angle on the topic

3. Writers can develop paragraphs and support main ideas by giving _____.

   a. other possible thesis statements

   b. possible readers' opinions

   c. examples, descriptions, and explanations from experts

4. A good way to anticipate possible reader questions is to _____.

   a. pretend that you are the reader and list questions about each idea

   b. interview all potential readers and use their questions as you write

   c. direct the reader to think of questions as he or she reads your essay

5. A good example of an expert to include information from is _____.

   a. a talk show host

   b. a scholar or researcher in the field

   c. a person with general interest in the topic who comments on an online message board or in a chat room

Name _____   **Date** _____

1. Match each word with its definition. (5 points)

___	1. temple	a.	digging, usually to recover something
___	2. shrine	b.	decay
___	3. ruins	c.	qualifying an argument
___	4. relic	d.	suitable for a burial
___	5. provisioning	e.	too many to count
___	6. excavation	f.	place of devotion to a saint or a god
___	7. speculation	g.	remains of something old or decayed
___	8. funerary	h.	an object that has survived passing time
___	9. deterioration	i.	place of religious worship
___	10. innumerable	j.	unproven theory about the unknown

2. Number the sentences in order. (5 points)

____ Then you can see how the lines resemble animals and geometric shapes.

____ They wonder how and why the ancient Nazca culture made these incredible pictures.

____ The giant Nazca lines in Peru are too big to be seen in their entirety from the ground.

____ Many people have speculated about them.

____ Therefore, it is necessary to view them from an airplane.

3. Circle the letter of the correct answer. (5 points)

1. Which of these sentences is correct?

   a. The Nazca lines in Peru may be built by the ancient Nazcans as a landing strip for visitors from outer space.

   b. The Nazca lines in Peru may have built by the ancient Nazcans as a landing strip for visitors from outer space.

   c. The Nazca lines in Peru may have been built by the ancient Nazcans as a landing strip for visitors from outer space.

2. Which of these sentences is correct?

   a. The giant stone statues on Easter Island must have been carved with sharp tools.

   b. The giant stone statues on Easter Island must be carved with sharp tools.

   c. The giant stone statues on Easter Island must be deduced to have been carved with sharp tools.

3. Which of these sentences is correct?

   a. It is believed that in ancient times there were only 2,000 people on Easter Island to move the giant statues, but possibly there were definitely more.

   b. It is believed that in ancient times there were only 2,000 people on Easter Island to move the giant statues, but possibly there were probably more.

   c. It is believed that in ancient times there were only 2,000 people on Easter Island to move the giant statues, but there were possibly more.

4. Which of these sentences indicates speculation?

   a. It has been proven that dinosaurs all died within a short period of time.

   b. It is possible to deduce that dinosaurs all died within a short period of time.

   c. Without a doubt, the evidence points to the fact that dinosaurs all died within a short period of time.

5. Which of these statements used as supporting material is not a fact?

   a. Loch Ness, where the Loch Ness monster has been sighted, is located in Scotland.

   b. Many people believe they have seen the Loch Ness monster, so we can deduce that it actually exists.

   c. Loch Ness is a large lake that attracts thousands of tourists each year.

4. Read this text and then answer the following questions. (5 points)

One of the most intriguing unsolved mysteries of our times is the strange appearance of crop circles (also sometimes called "crop formations") in fields all over the world. They have been reported in virtually every country in the world, with the exception of China and South Africa. Most of them occur—or at least are reported—in the United Kingdom. Crop circles are imprinted designs—usually circles, but sometimes squares, triangles, and other shapes and patterns—that appear in farmers' fields. They usually appear in fields of wheat and corn, but they have been found in fields of barley, oats, grass, and even snow. They tend to appear mysteriously overnight. The next morning a farmer might go out to the field and find the grains or the grass completely flattened into perfect circles or more complex designs. "I couldn't believe my eyes," said Graham Bannier, who owns a farm in the northern region of England. "The corn was flattened into these big circles. Not broken or destroyed—just flattened, as if it were growing horizontally. I was sure it was a hoax. You know, some kids playing a joke. But as I looked around, I realized that there was no path into or out of the circle. There was no way that somebody could have brought in equipment and left all of the surrounding corn rows entirely undisturbed."

Researchers have been studying the mysterious crop circles for many years. The earliest circles reported in England date back to 1647. Since then, circles have appeared with increasing frequency and, throughout the 1990s, with increasing complexity in designs. Scientists who have tested plant and soil samples from within crop circles have noticed physical changes to plant cell walls and to soil. Other researchers have noticed that electronic equipment seems to malfunction inside crop circles. For example, cell phones, batteries, cameras, and watches do not seem to work well or at all. Some people also report feeling physically ill or strange when standing inside a crop circle. They may feel headaches, dizziness, and nausea.

One theory that scientists have come up with to explain these strange effects on equipment and on people is that strong electromagnetic field distortions in the circles may have caused them.

Despite years of research, scientists still have not definitively been able to explain the cause of crop circles. Until they do, other theories—hoaxes, spacecrafts landing, energies deep in the earth, military experimentation—will likely continue to circulate.

1. What sentence best describes the writer's purpose?

   a. To persuade people to study crop circles.

   b. To describe crop circles and explain speculations about their causes.

   c. To inform people about the danger of crop circles.

2. What type of supporting material is found in paragraph one, sentences 2-5?

   a. anecdotes

   b. facts

   c. statistics

3. What type of supporting material is found in paragraph one, sentences 8-14?

   a. anecdote

   b. fact

   c. statistic

4. What type of supporting material is found in paragraph two, sentence 3?

   a. anecdote

   b. fact

   c. statistic

5. Which of these statements describes a speculation mentioned in the article?

   a. Crop circles have been reported in virtually every country in the world, with the exception of China and South Africa.

   b. When Graham Bannier discovered crop circles in his field, he was certain they were a hoax.

   c. Strong electromagnetic field distortions in the crop circles may have affected mechanical equipment and people.

5. Complete the following sentences (5 points)

1. Here is an example of supporting material used in a paragraph: "As recently as 1999, campers in the forests of Oregon were startled to see a large, hairy creature that looked part human and part animal thrash through the bushes not far from their campsite." This type of supporting material is

   _____.

   a. a statistic

   b. an anecdote

   c. a fact

2. Here is an example of supporting material used in a paragraph: "Since the first reported sighting of Bigfoot in 1924, police records for the states of Washington, Oregon, and Idaho show nearly 100 reported Bigfoot sightings." This type of supporting material is _____.

   a. a statistic

   b. an anecdote

   c. an opinion of the author

3. Examples used as supporting material are generally _____.

   a. lengthy personal stories

   b. representative people, qualities, rules, or events

   c. numbers or parts of numbers by which we can measure facts

4. Statistics used as supporting material are generally _____.

   a. numbers or parts of collections of numbers by which we can measure facts

   b. fictional, if the author thinks that most people are likely to agree

   c. mathematical problems

5. A fact used as supporting material generally _____.

   a. conveys the author's opinion on the issue

   b. is speculative

   c. is a true piece of information or an event that has happened

Name _____   **Date** _____

1. Match each word with its definition. (5 points)

____ 1. ambiguity   a. being adult

____ 2. tumultuous   b. made longer

____ 3. maturity   c. confusion

____ 4. socialization   d. upsetting

____ 5. transitional   e. celebrations or special events

____ 6. crisis   f. the state of being unclear

____ 7. prolonged   g. teaching behavior

____ 8. adolescence   h. a time of difficulty

____ 9. festivities   i. in a period of change

____ 10. turmoil   j. period of time between childhood and adulthood

2. Number the sentences in order. (5 points)

____ The ceremony typically occurs when the child turns thirteen.

____ The names of these ceremonies indicate whether they are for boys or for girls; Bar Mitzvah means "Son of the Commandments" and Bat Mitzvah means "Daughter of the Commandments."

____ In the Jewish religious tradition, the Bar and Bat Mitzvah ceremonies celebrate a boy or a girl's becoming an adult.

____ Later, he or she celebrates with friends and family at a big party.

____ First the child reads from the Torah (the Five Books of Moses).

3. Circle the letter of the correct answer. (5 points)

1. Which of these sentences is correct?

     a. Adolescents may be more maturity physically than emotionally.

     b. Adolescents may have more mature physically then emotionally.

     c. Adolescents may be more mature physically than emotionally.

2. Which of these sentences is correct?

     a. Many people feel that children learn gender roles through socialization.

     b. Many people feel that children learn gender roles through socialize.

     c. Many people feel that children learn gender roles through social.

3. Which of these sentences is correct?

   a. The ambiguous of the onset of old age is of interest to many sociologists.

   b. The ambiguity of the onset of old age is of interest to many sociologists.

   c. The ambigument of the onset of old age is of interest to many sociologists.

4. Which of these sentences correctly cites a source?

   a. As some people have said, rites of passage during the teenage years often make young men and women feel fully included in the community for the first time.

   b. As indicated in the article "The Cultural Significance of Rites of Passage," rites of passage during the teenage years often make young men and women feel fully included in the community for the first time (Miller, Liu and Wang, 1998: 32-33).

   c. Rites of passage during the teenage years often make young men and women feel fully included in the community for the first time (Miller, Liu and Wang).

5. Here is an example of a topic sentence for a paragraph: "North American culture has several rites of passage that may not be formally recognized with ceremonies, but which are considered important steps to adulthood nevertheless." Which of these sentences is a good bridge sentence?

   a. We might learn more about the significance of these smaller-scale rites of passage by talking with young people about ways that they personally marked these milestones.

   b. Obtaining a driver's license or registering to vote are two specific examples of rites of passage.

   c. These smaller-scale rites of passage include the recognition of new civic or community privileges and responsibilities.

4. Read this text and then answer the following questions. (5 points)

In Latin America, and in Hispanic communities in the United States, the Quinceañera is an important ceremony to honor a girl's fifteenth birthday. The name of the event means "15 years": *quince* is Spanish for *fifteen*, and *años* means *years*. This year is traditionally the year that a girl becomes a woman, makes her debut into society, and becomes ready for adult responsibilities like work and marriage. Fifteen years old today might seem quite young for marriage, but this tradition originated with the ancient Mayan and Aztec cultures, and at one time it was common for girls of fifteen to begin considering marriage. Many of the old traditions of this ceremony have carried over into today's modern times, even if girls no longer marry at this young age. The ceremony itself can resemble a wedding: the girl typically wears a white or a light-colored dress, a tiara (a kind of crown) on her head, and carries flowers. She also dances the first dance (usually a waltz) with her father and then dances with the other male guests in turn.

Another tradition that may carry over from the past is the changing of flat-heeled shoes into high heels, to mark the entrance into womanhood. Yet another tradition is the giving of a porcelain doll to a younger sister. This act symbolizes leaving childhood behind—in this case, leaving it to her sister. These are modern times, and like most cultural rites of passage, the quinceañera is changing bit by bit in order to adapt. Some of the older traditions have been abandoned. The Internet has become a resource for planning a quinceañera; this resource can help facilitate planning and bring people together, but it can also depersonalize the event. Additionally, today there may be more of an emphasis on throwing a big party and less education about the young woman's past heritage and future adult responsibilities. However, judging by the amount of traditions that have endured, the anticipation of this important event has probably not diminished at all since the days of the Mayans and Aztecs. Young women entering a new phase of life still walk on the paths of their ancestors.

1. What sentence best describes the writer's purpose?

   a. To argue that the quinceañera has become too modern and lost many important traditions.

   b. To inform readers how to plan a good quinceañera.

   c. To explain the significance and some traditions of the quinceañera.

2. What type of supporting material is *not* used in this paragraph?

   a. anecdotes

   b. facts

   c. examples

3. How many illustrations of older traditions still practiced today does the writer give?

   a. six

   b. four

   c. three

4. How many illustrations of modern changes to the quinceañera does the writer give?

   a. four

   b. one

   c. two

5. Which sentence best summarizes the writer's interpretation of the supporting material?

   a. It is too bad that so many of the older traditions have not survived into modern times.

   b. So many of the older traditions have survived into modern times that the basic importance of and excitement about the ceremony probably has not changed.

   c. The quinceañera is as important today as any other cultural event.

5. Complete the following sentences (5 points)

1. The bridge sentence of a paragraph _____.

   a. links the author's opinion to an expert's

   b. explains the main idea and connects it to the supporting material

   c. connects the thesis to the first body paragraph

2. The type of sentence that follows the supporting material in a paragraph and explains how it relates to the topic sentence is _____.

   a. an interpretation

   b. a conclusion

   c. a bridge sentence

3. Another word for *interpretation* is _____.

   a. fact

   b. analysis

   c. conclusion

4. The purpose of the topic sentence of a paragraph is to _____.

   a. state the author's thesis

   b. present an interpretation

   c. express the main idea of the paragraph

5. The different types of supporting material you choose for your paragraph _____.

   a. should be included in equal amounts

   b. can be omitted when a topic sentence and interpretation are sufficient

   c. can be used in combination or in isolation, and in varying amounts, depending on your topic and purpose

Name _____   **Date** _____

1. Match each word with its definition. (5 points)

___ 1. to decipher   a. happening again and again

___ 2. traumatic   b. relating to the body

___ 3. the unconscious   c. without thinking

___ 4. to reflect   d. an implicit comparison

___ 5. physiological   e. to read or interpret something ambiguous

___ 6. unconsciously   f. physically or emotionally painful

___ 7. metaphor   g. to make something apparent; to show

___ 8. recurring   h. relating to the mind or emotions

___ 9. psychological   i. something representing a thought /feeling

___ 10. symbol   j. division of the mind not subject to conscious
                                    control

2. Organize the notes below into an outline for a paragraph. Use general-to-specific divided organization. (5 points)

Notes

Psychological interpretations   Dreams

The brain stem sends signals to the cortex, which turns signals into dream stories

Freud's theory of the unconscious   Physiological aspects

A recurring dream about a house might symbolize your personal health.

People you see randomly in the day may be stored as memory and transmitted to you in your dreams later.

Outline:

1 _____

   2 _____

      3 _____

         4 _____

   2 _____

      3 _____

         4 _____

3. Circle the letter of the correct answer. (5 points)

1. Which of these sentences is correct?

   a. Last night I had a dream flying.

   b. Last night I had a dream about flying.

   c. Last night I dreamed flying.

2. Which of these sentences is correct?

   a. Dreams may be warnings sent to us by the unconsciously.

   b. Dreams may be unconsciously warnings sent to us.

   c. Dreams may be warnings sent to us by the unconscious.

3. Which of these sentences is correct?

   a. Some experts say that recurring dreams can predict the future.

   b. Some experts say that recur dreams can predict the future.

   c. Some experts say that dreams can recur the future.

4. Which of these sentences is correct?

   a. Some physiological effects of nightmares include fear and emotional distress.

   b. Some psychological effects of nightmares include trembling and sweating.

   c. Some physiological effects of nightmares include trembling and sweating.

5. Which of these sentences is correct?

   a. It is commonly thought that cars in dreams symbolize where you are going in life.

   b. It is commonly thought that cars in dreams symbol where you are going in life.

   c. It is commonly thought that cars in dreams symbolic where you are going in life.

4. Read this text and then answer the following questions. (5 points)

Are you superstitious? Do you prefer not to travel on Friday the 13th? Do you avoid stepping on cracks in the sidewalk? Do you make a wish when you see a falling star? A superstition is a belief in supernatural powers, or a fear, usually irrational, of the unknown. People all over the world, in all cultures, have various superstitions. In North America, there are many superstitions associated with good luck and bad luck, and these superstitions seem to be widely followed even by those who claim not to be superstitious. The superstitions about good luck are perhaps more widely accepted; many North Americans have some small rituals to invite good luck for an important event. For example, many people carry a lucky item, such as a horseshoe or a rabbit's foot or something of personal significance. Others may instinctively reach down to pick up a penny that they find on the ground—but only if it is shiny or if it has the "heads" side facing up. Superstitions about bad luck, on the other hand, are often scoffed at by people who claim not to be superstitious. They say that a black cat crossing your path is no indication of bad luck, that the number 13 is not inherently cursed, and that although yawning without covering your mouth may be impolite, it does not invite the devil into your body. Nevertheless, a great many people follow superstitions that are believed to ward off bad luck. For example, a recent news magazine show set up a hidden camera near a ladder that was positioned to block off a large section of sidewalk. Pedestrians would have to either walk under the ladder or around it, going partly out into the street. Most people seemed to follow the superstition that walking under a ladder brings bad luck. They walked around it—even though the TV show producers had placed some cash under the ladder as a temptation. In the end, only one person tried to take the money—and he quickly reached his arm under the ladder to grab it, in order to avoid walking under it. Perhaps people who insist they are not superstitious are more superstitious than they would like to admit. Perhaps they do not like the idea that the unknown can be so frightening.

1. What sentence best describes the writer's purpose?

   a. To describe how some superstitions for good luck and bad luck in North America are widely believed.

   b. To argue that more people in North America follow superstitions for good luck than for bad luck.

   c. To explain how North Americans are more superstitious than people from other cultures.

2. How is this paragraph organized?

   a. general-to-specific top-down organization

   b. general-to-specific divided organization

   c. chronological organization

3. Which of these sentences is the topic sentence?

   a. Are you superstitious?

   b. A superstition is a belief in supernatural powers, or a fear, usually irrational, of the unknown.

   c. In North America, there are many superstitions associated with good luck and bad luck, and these superstitions seem to be widely followed even by those who claim not to be superstitious.

4. How many examples and facts does the writer provide?

   a. two

   b. five

   c. four

5. Which of these sentences is the most general?

   a. In the end, only one person tried to take the money—and he quickly reached his arm under the ladder to grab it, in order to avoid walking under it.

   b. People all over the world, in all cultures, have various superstitions.

   c. Others may instinctively reach down to pick up a penny that they find on the ground—but only if it is shiny or if it has the "heads" side facing up.

5. Complete the following sentences (5 points)

1. "Drawing" or diagramming your ideas when you plan an essay is useful because _____.

   a. sometimes words are not useful

   b. there is only one correct way to organize an essay

   c. many organizational patterns can be represented visually; you can see relationships between ideas

2. Top-down organization looks like a set of stairs because _____.

   a. each idea in the paragraph moves one step down to show decreasing importance

   b. each idea in the paragraph moves one step down in generality

   c. each idea in the paragraph moves one step up to show increasing importance

3. Divided organization looks like two sets of stairs because _____.

   a. it moves from general to specific ideas for two parts of a topic sentence

   b. it moves from general to specific ideas for two thesis statements

   c. it moves from general to specific ideas to show them in increasing importance followed by decreasing importance

4. In a divided organization outline, level 2 sentences indicate _____.

   a. very specific facts or illustrations

   b. different parts of the topic sentence

   c. more specific information about the facts and illustrations

5. In divided organization, level 3 sentences indicate _____.

   a. very specific facts or illustrations

   b. different parts of the topic sentence

   c. more specific information about the facts and illustrations

Name _____   **Date** _____

1. Match each word with its definition. (5 points)

___	1. refinements	a.	start
___	2. harmonious	b.	implement
___	3. bargaining	c.	discussion
___	4. deliberation	d.	tell others
___	5. lessened	e.	political
___	6. pass the word	f.	improvements
___	7. management style	g.	persuading
___	8. initiate	h.	being in agreement
___	9. sensitive	i.	a way of getting work done in a company
___	10. accomplish	j.	made smaller or less important

2. Using the thesis statement as a guide, organize the notes below into an outline for a causal chain essay. (5 points)

<u>Thesis Statement:</u> Studying a foreign language for many years in school can lead to increased job opportunities later on.

<u>Notes</u>
Increased proficiency in the language
Increased interest in the culture can lead to a desire or opportunity to travel there
Job opportunities, either in that culture or elsewhere.
Studying a foreign language for many years in school
total immersion in the culture and near-fluency in the language
Increased interest in the culture / place in which the language is spoken.

<u>Outline:</u>
I.   a–f (thesis statement)

II. a–b–c: _____

III. d–e–f: _____

IV. Conclusion

3. Circle the letter of the correct answer. (5 points)

1. Which of these sentences is correct?

   a. Cross-cultural miscommunications in the workplace result a lack of knowledge about cultural differences.

   b. Cross-cultural miscommunications in the workplace result from a lack of knowledge about cultural differences.

   c. Cross-cultural miscommunications in the workplace are the result from a lack of knowledge about cultural differences.

2. Which of these sentences is *incorrect?*

   a. Because of a lack of English proficiency, many highly trained professionals from other countries may have difficulty finding work in their field in the U.S.

   b. Many highly-trained professionals from other countries may have difficulty finding work in their field in the U.S. because of their lack of English proficiency.

   c. Many highly-trained professionals from other countries lack English proficiency as a result of their difficulty finding work in their field in the U.S.

3. Which of these sentences is correct?

   a. A lack of knowledge about cross-cultural differences in business can result from miscommunications, which in turn can result from employee frustration.

   b. A lack of knowledge about cross-cultural differences in business can lead to miscommunications, which in turn can result in employee frustration.

   c. A lack of knowledge about cross-cultural differences in business can lead to miscommunications, which in turn can result from employee frustration.

4. Here is an example statement from an essay on business practices in different cultures: "In Latin America, businesspeople usually converse socially for some time before getting down to business." What inference can be made from this statement?

   a. Latin American businesspeople may find it confusing or impolite if people immediately begin to discuss business matters.

   b. Latin American businesspeople have the only correct way to do business.

   c. Latin American businesspeople are the only people who follow this procedure.

5. Here is a statement from an essay on business practices in North America: "An employer is not legally allowed to ask an applicant about his or her age, marital status, or religious affiliation." What inference can be made from this statement?

   a. An international job applicant might not be able to obtain a job with a North American company.

   b. An international job applicant should volunteer this information anyway.

   c. Businesses in other countries may not have the same law; therefore, foreign applicants should be aware of it in case a prospective employers asks these questions illegally.

4. Read this text and then answer the following questions. (5 points)

Companies have increasingly found themselves enjoying greater success as a result of focusing on quality of life issues for their employees. One company in particular, DCR Systems, stands out as an example of this phenomenon, and as a case study of how greater returns in a company are a direct result from greater employee satisfaction. In 2000, *Quick Business* magazine voted DCR Systems as the company with the highest reported level of employee satisfaction. At the time that the survey was conducted, many employees reported a new policy that the company had implemented, contributing money toward tuition for continuing education or evening classes for their employees. "DCR Systems definitely contributed to my professional development, and it continues to do so," says Barbara Worth, who first entered the company as an administrative assistant and is now Director of Finance.

Barbara also indicated that the professional development initiatives had followed from previous changes designed to help employees balance their professional and personal lives. In previous years, the company had installed a number of on-site services such as a drycleaners, a gym, a yoga studio, and a food court that offers healthy food choices. That surge of facilities had resulted from the company's first on-site resource: a daycare center to accommodate the needs of working parents with very young children. "DCR Systems has considered itself family-focused from its inception," says founder and CEO Kenneth Schwartz. "We recognize the fact that an employee who is constantly worried about his or her child is not going to be as productive at work. This way, parents know where their children are, they know who they're with, and they can even go and visit the child on a break if they need to. There's no long commute to a daycare center, so the employee is almost always on time and rarely needs to leave early." But even if an employee did need to arrive late or leave early, due to childcare responsibilities or other matters, the flextime system, which originally gave rise to the idea for a daycare center, would accommodate such scheduling needs. DCR Systems is a model for how a company can continue being flexible in responding to its employees' needs and profiting financially from their employees' satisfaction. Other companies would do well to study this model. Quality of life in the workplace will no doubt continue to be an issue of increasing importance as people continue struggling to meet competing demands in our increasingly fast-paced and complex world.

1. What sentence best describes the writer's purpose?

   a. To describe causes and effects of the increasing attention being paid to employees' quality of life in the workplace.

   b. To argue that companies need to pay more attention to quality of life issues for employees.

   c. To narrate a personal experience about improved conditions in the workplace.

2. How is this paragraph organized?

   a. As a causal chain beginning with the initial cause and working up to the final result.

   b. As a causal chain beginning with the final result and working back to the initial cause.

   c. A causal chain listing causes and effects in order of importance.

3. How many intermediate steps are listed in this causal chain?

   a. four

   b. six

   c. three

4. How many causes are listed in this text? How many effects?

   a. 1 cause, 1 effect

   b. 4 causes, 1 effect

   c. 5 causes, 5 effects

5. Which sentence best summarizes this text?

    a. If a company doesn't follow all of the steps that DCR Systems did to improve the workplace environment, their employees might leave to work at DCR Systems.

    b. Many companies are making changes to improve the workplace and meet the needs of their employees.

    c. Employee satisfaction, which can be achieved through many different steps, results in greater success for the company, as illustrated by the model of DCR Systems.

5. Complete the following sentences (5 points)

1. To *infer* something is to _____.

    a. state something indirectly in speaking or writing

    b. state something directly in speaking or writing

    c. use context and existing material to guess at what is not directly stated

2. *Consensus* is _____.

    a. a formal debate about an issue

    b. a style of decision-making that involves everyone in a group and has the goal of working toward an agreement

    c. consenting to give your opinion on an issue

3. The diagram a → b → c illustrates _____.

    a. a simple causal relationship

    b. a causal chain

    c. a cause, effect, and conclusion

4. If a causal chain is the subject of an entire essay, then it is necessary to have _____.

    a. concrete evidence for each step in the chain

    b. a repertoire of organizational patterns

    c. enough intermediate steps to develop into at least two body paragraphs

5. A second way to organize a causal chain essay is to _____.

    a. compare causes with effects

    b. begin with the final result and work back to the initial cause

    c. begin in the middle of the chain and work outward to each cause and effect

Name _____   **Date** _____

1. Match each word with its definition. (5 points)

____ 1. hazards   a. not harmful to the environment

____ 2. innovative   b. saving

____ 3. in compliance   c. produce

____ 4. green   d. doesn't use too much energy

____ 5. generate   e. meeting guidelines

____ 6. convert   f. dangers

____ 7. energy-efficient   g. material to be used for something else

____ 8. conservation   h. public services like electricity, gas, water

____ 9. source   i. new

____ 10. utilities   j. change

2. Number the sentences in order. (5 points)

____ Other questions to ask yourself would be: do I want to study in an urban, suburban, or rural environment? How long are the classes? What resources are available?

____ Finally, you will probably need two or three letters of recommendation from people who know you or your work well; be sure to request these letters far enough in advance so that your references can compose thoughtful, accurate letters.

____ Your next step should be to select the schools that most fit your interests and request application materials.

____ To begin, you should think about your goals and conduct careful research about schools and their courses of study.

____ There are several preliminary steps to follow in order to apply for a university program and maximize your chances of being accepted into the program of your choice.

3. Circle the letter of the correct answer. (5 points)

1. Which of these sentences is correct?

    a. Different types of wind turbines are show in the following diagrams.

    b. Different types of wind turbines are shown in the following diagrams.

    c. Different types of wind turbines show in the following diagrams.

2. Which of these sentences is correct?

   a. Solar energy absorbers are face south.

   b. Solar energy absorbers faced south.

   c. Solar energy absorbers are faced south.

3. Which of these sentences is correct?

   a. Companies involved with solar energy must be in compliance with requirements for product safety and building codes.

   b. Companies involved with solar energy must be compliance with requirements for product safety and building codes.

   c. Companies involved with solar energy must be comply with requirements for product safety and building codes.

4. Here is an example statement from an essay: "Several different kinds of alternative energy sources generate clean electricity." Which statement correctly rewrites the sentence in the passive voice?

   a. Clean electricity generates by several different kinds of alternative energy sources.

   b. Clean electricity is generated by several different kinds of alternative energy sources.

   c. Several different kinds of alternative energy sources are generated by clean electricity.

5. Which sentence is the best way to describe the parts or components of something?

   a. New roofs designed for solar energy are positioned with a combination of regular asphalt shingles and photovoltaic shingles that protect the roof like regular shingles while generating electricity.

   b. New roofs designed for solar energy give a combination of regular asphalt shingles and photovoltaic shingles that protect the roof like regular shingles while generating electricity.

   c. New roofs designed for solar energy involve a combination of regular asphalt shingles and photovoltaic shingles that protect the roof like regular shingles while generating electricity.

4. Read this text and then answer the following questions. (5 points)

Many people, when they think of conserving energy, feel that it must take a tremendous effort. They may feel that there is very little they can do without installing expensive solar panels, heat pumps, or other expensive devices. They may also feel that they can't make a difference. However, you can begin conserving energy in your home today, just by making small changes that cost no or little money. Begin by becoming aware of how much electricity you use for your day-to-day tasks. Do you turn off lights when you leave the room? Do you put your computer on "sleep mode" when you're not using it? Do you stand for a long time with the refrigerator door open, wondering what to eat? Do you run the dishwasher or do laundry without full loads? Raising your awareness of your energy usage for everyday activities, and beginning to change your behaviors, is an important step in the process of conserving energy. After you have modified your energy use for some of your daily activities, look at your living environment, room by room. You might want to take notes as you carry out this inspection. What kind of heating system or air conditioning system do you use? Are you turning the heat or air-conditioning up high? If so, you're using more electricity than you may need to. Lower the heat in the winter and put on extra clothes; also, check windows for cracks where cold can come in, and check your insulation. In the summer, use the air conditioning only when you need to, and close window drapes and shades to help cool the rooms. Finally, consider investing in a few low-cost "green" products to help you to conserve energy on a daily basis. There are many products on the market, and the selection process can seem like a daunting task. Therefore, you should think about your daily activities and your home and prioritize two to four areas that you could improve upon with the aid of some inexpensive products. For example, energy-efficient lighting is an affordable, easy investment for most people. Compact fluorescent light bulbs use approximately 75% less electricity than regular light bulbs; moreover, they can last up to seven years. Another example of an affordable investment is weather-stripping, sealing, and caulking doors and windows where hot air escapes or cold air comes in. If you follow these basic steps in the process of learning to conserve energy in your home, you may be inspired to do more and more—especially when you see the savings on your utility bills! You may feel that you are only one person and that you or your family alone does not consume enough electricity to affect anything. However, if everyone followed these basic steps, their combined efforts would make a tremendous difference.

1. What sentence best describes the writer's purpose?

   a. To persuade people to make dramatic lifestyle changes in order to conserve energy.

   b. To describe the process of how one can begin conserving energy in their home.

   c. To warn people about what will happen if we do not work together to conserve energy.

2. How is this paragraph organized?

   a. As a chronological description.

   b. As a structural description.

   c. As a cause and effect description.

3. How many steps are listed in this process?

   a. four

   b. six

   c. three

4. Who is most likely the writer's intended audience?

   a. People who know a great deal about energy conservation and have already been implementing some basic changes in their lifestyles.

   b. People who know very little about energy conservation and may be intimidated by the concept of making changes in their lifestyles or doubtful that they can effect change.

   c. People who are reasonably informed about energy conservation and are likely to completely disagree with the writer.

5. Which sentence best summarizes this text?

   a. By following some basic steps toward raising awareness of energy consumption and making slight modifications to daily activities and the home, everyone can contribute to energy conservation.

   b. By following some basic steps toward raising awareness of energy consumption and making slight modifications to daily activities and the home, everyone will be inspired to make major changes and invest in more expensive products to aid energy conservation.

   c. Even if they follow some basic steps toward raising awareness of energy consumption and making slight modifications to daily activities and the home, many people still may feel that they cannot contribute much to energy conservation.

5. Complete the following sentences (5 points)

1. Considering your audience is important when you write about a process because _____.

   a. it helps you to guess what grade you will get

   b. it helps you to anticipate your audience's own writing

   c. it helps you to determine what they already know and what they need to know about your subject

2. Some transition words commonly used in chronological process descriptions are _____.

   a. although, on the one hand, on the other hand, while, however

   b. first, second, next, finally

   c. since, because, as a result, therefore

3. The thesis statement in an essay describing a process usually _____.

   a. describes the entire process from start to finish

   b. announces what process you will describe and how you will describe it

   c. states the end of the process and works back to the beginning

4. A type of process that describes and/or analyzes an object or event in order to determine the organization is called a _____.

   a. structural description

   b. chronological description

   c. outline description

5. Passive voice and process descriptions are common features of _____.

   a. creative writing

   b. argument essays

   c. scientific writing

Name _____   **Date** _____

1. Match each word with its definition. (5 points)

___	1. functional	a.	drawing or painting of a person / face
___	2. perjorative	b.	simple; at an early stage of development
___	3. sculpture	c.	the parts forming a whole
___	4. primitive	d.	strangely unfamiliar or unusual
___	5. communal	e.	a three-dimensional figure, often of clay
___	6. composition	f.	having a use
___	7. surrealistic	g.	demonstrating personal expression
___	8. exotic	h.	reflecting interest and values of society
___	9. portrait	i.	negative
___	10. individualistic	j.	with dreamlike or unreal qualities

2. Number the sentences in order. (5 points)

___ Folk art can also come in many different forms, including paintings, drawings, sculpture, furniture, needlework, and pottery, to name just a few.

___ Despite confusion over the term and its examples, a growing number of folk art museums and folk art gallery exhibits suggest that there is increasing interest in the genre and that we ought to take it more seriously.

___ *Folk art* is a term that is often misapplied or misunderstood, perhaps because it can come in so many different forms.

___ The term *folk art* can also be used to describe craft techniques that have been passed down through generations, or to describe art produced by an untrained artisan that reflects a region, a culture, or a religious tradition.

___ Before explaining the various forms it can come in, we should first establish the fact that the basic definition of *folk art* is that it is art produced by a self-trained artist—that is, an artist who has received no formal training and is an "outsider" to the elite art community.

3. Circle the letter of the correct answer. (5 points)

1. Here is the first sentence of an introduction paragraph for an essay: "In her article 'Folk Art as a Window into Worlds,' Jane Newman describes the anthropological significance of folk art from different cultures." What technique does the writer use to generate reader interest?

   a. Background information

   b. Summary

   c. Definition

2. Here are the first sentences of an introduction paragraph for an essay: "Over the past few years, folk art has generated increasing amounts of interest in the art world at large. However, the art world's interest in folk art goes back earlier than we think, and has influenced more artists than we may be aware of." What technique does the writer use to generate reader interest?

   a. Background information

   b. Summary

   c. Definition

3. Which of these sentences most effectively describes or analyzes a work of art?

   a. The painting called "Starry Night" uses sad colors with some happy ones.

   b. Van Gogh's painting "Starry Night" transmits a feeling of hope in the midst of loneliness through its combination of dark and light colors.

   c. "Starry Night," painted by Van Gogh, is a response to something.

4. Which of these sentences most effectively describes or analyzes a work of art?

   a. Monet's "Water Lilies" is a painting that has no use.

   b. Monet's painting "Water Lilies" is beautiful to look at, but it doesn't have any cultural or religious uses.

   c. Monet's painting "Water Lilies" is an expression of art for its own sake rather than art that is functional.

5. Which of these quotations would be the best to use in an introduction to an essay about inner-city art museums?

   a. "Let the people come to experience art first-hand, to see beauty where they might not have looked for it before." (Ernest Johnson, a city mayor)

   b. "Nothing is less real than realism. Details are confusing." (Georgia O'Keeffe, American artist).

   c. "Genius is one percent inspiration and ninety-nine percent perspiration." (Albert Einstein)

4. Read this text and then answer the following questions. (5 points)

"It's all about the process, not about the product," says Gail Metzker, who is up to her elbows in paint. She has been teaching a group of adults—professionals, homemakers, parents—to finger paint on long pieces of butcher paper. The room is buzzing with activity and laughter, and there is not a child around. One woman is wiping away tears as she regards her finished painting. Another man frowns as he looks at his before ripping it into pieces. Gail Metzker goes over to both the man and the woman and says a few comforting words. The two students look relieved. This art class is not about perfecting technique or creating a masterpiece. It's about feelings—expressing them and exploring them by creating visual representations of them. And Gail Metzker is not a fine artist or a master teacher; she is an art therapist. Art therapy is the practice of helping people use art to reconnect with their thoughts and feelings— sometimes painful ones. Some people may look at the scene in Gail Metzker's room and think that it's just adults playing like children. The approaches and the benefits may not be immediately obvious to an outsider. However, by tracing the history of art therapy, seeing how Gail Metzker's classroom techniques are founded in psychotherapy, and hearing personal testimonies from Gail's students, the benefits of art therapy will become clear.

1. What sentence best describes the writer's purpose in the essay that will develop from this introduction?

    a. To persuade the reader to take up art therapy.

    b. To describe the history, techniques, and testimonies of art therapy in order to help people see its benefits.

    c. To explain the process of how art therapy is practiced.

2. What technique does the writer use to create reader interest?

    a. Beginning with background information.

    b. Beginning with a quotation.

    c. Beginning with a definition.

3. What other technique is used in this introduction to create reader interest?

    a. background information

    b. summary

    c. definition

4. What is the thesis statement of this introduction?

    a. However, by tracing the history of art therapy, seeing how Gail Metzker's classroom techniques are founded in psychotherapy, and hearing personal testimonies from Gail's students, the benefits of art therapy will become clear.

    b. Art therapy is the practice of helping people use art to reconnect with their thoughts and feelings—sometimes painful ones.

    c. There is no thesis statement.

5. Who is most likely the writer's intended audience?

    a. Psychiatrists and art therapists.

    b. Students in art therapy classes.

    c. People who do not know much about art therapy.

5. Complete the following sentences (5 points)

1. The critical thinking skill of applying what you've learned involves _____.

   a. asking for help in understanding new concepts

   b. applying new concepts to a familiar situation

   c. applying familiar concepts to a familiar situation

2. A successful introduction for an essay should *not* _____.

   a. prepare readers for what is to come

   b. create a high level of interest in the topic

   c. include supporting points and specific examples

3. A good conclusion of an essay _____.

   a. makes the reader feel that the thesis statement has been developed and that the essay has been brought to a close.

   b. leaves the reader with a sense of interest and mystery about what the writer's opinion really is.

   c. restates the thesis statement in the same words

4. One way to write a conclusion is to _____.

   a. end with a quotation or a definition

   b. include a challenging thought on the topic with some new information to think about

   c. provide background information on the topic

5. Three common types of introductions are _____.

   a. general-to-specific, chronological, problem-solution

   b. historical, scientific, creative

   c. effective, ineffective, somewhat effective

Name _____   **Date** _____

1. Match each word with its definition. (5 points)

___	1. constituency	a.	community of plants, animals, organisms
___	2. humanism	b.	rightness or purity of behavior
___	3. conscience	c.	people represented by an elected official
___	4. authentic	d.	related to living things and environments
___	5. morality	e.	a judge's office in a courthouse
___	6. ecosystem	f.	a sense of right and wrong
___	7. spokesperson	g.	faithfulness to a person or a cause
___	8. ecological	h.	person speaking publicly about a cause
___	9. chamber	i.	real, true, or believable
___	10. loyalty	j.	thought system concerned with people's interests, values, and well-being

2. Number the sentences in order. (5 points)

___ We anticipate many problems resulting from the development of this new branch of the national Big Values chain.

___ We the undersigned are writing in protest of the proposed new Big Values store that is scheduled to open in Pleasant Town in May of 2002.

___ There is an additional concern about the proximity of the planned Big Values store to a children's playground; the constant traffic that would result from the megastore could pose safety hazards to the children, not to mention destroy the face of our town common.

___ The biggest problem we foresee is that it will cause the failure of most of many stores in Pleasant Town which are small, family-run businesses that cannot hope to compete with Big Values.

___ There is an undeveloped area of land off of a major highway that could be accessed by several towns, including Pleasant Town, without defacing any of them or directly harming their business. Perhaps this is a solution that you could consider.

3. Circle the letter of the correct answer. (5 points)

1. Which sentence is correct?

    a. "Wilderness" is considered be undeveloped and uninhabited regions.

    b. "Wilderness" is considering undeveloped and uninhabited regions.

    c. "Wilderness" is considered to be undeveloped and uninhabited regions

2. Which sentence uses abstract nouns?

a. It is the responsibility of all citizens to speak up for their needs and to let themselves be heard by their elected representatives.

b. All responsible citizens should speak up for their needs and let themselves be heard by their elected representatives.

c. In order to be responsible, all citizens should speak up for their needs and let themselves be heard by their elected representatives.

3. Which sentence uses a metaphor?

a. Trying to convince the lumber industry to slow down their clear-cutting of forests is like shouting in a desert.

b. It is shouting in a desert to try to convince the lumber industry to slow down their clear-cutting of forests.

c. Trying to convince the lumber industry to slow down their clear-cutting of forests can be compared to shouting in a desert.

4. "The mountains of bureaucracy rose up before us as we tried to protest the building of a giant Well-Smart Store in our town." How can this sentence best be interpreted?

a. It will be fairly easy to prevent the new store from being built.

b. Preventing the new store from being built will be a long, difficult process with many obstacles.

c. There may be some annoyances along the way in the process of preventing a new store from being built.

5. Which of the following definitions is a stipulated definition?

a. Among people who are involved in the environmental movement, the word *green* is not a color; it is a word used to describe something that is not harmful to the environment.

b. *Green* is a color on the spectrum between yellow and blue; it can also refer to a grassy common area in a city or town, and it can be used as an idiomatic expression to refer to someone who is new to or inexperienced about something.

c. *Green* most commonly refers to a color, but there can be many different shades of green depending on what you are referring to.

4. Read this text and then answer the following questions. (5 points)

One of the biggest problems facing our public schools today is the lack of attention paid to civics courses. The dictionary defines civics as a branch of political science concerned with the rights and duties of citizens. This type of definition, however, mystifies students—as well as many parents and educators—and it does not impart the full significance of the word. In the case of the problems in our public schools, therefore, I would like to redefine civics to be understood as the responsibility of educating and preparing young citizens for active participation in the American constitutional democracy. The skills learned in a rigorous civics class cannot be learned "naturally" or as by-products of other types of classes. Civics is an academic discipline in and of itself, and it is a moral obligation to ensure that students leave our public school system knowing exactly what it is and how it applies to their lives. They need to know how the government works, how to resolve conflicts, and how to be an active citizen capable of effecting change. A thorough civic education is crucial for the survival of our society, since a free society depends on the knowledge and virtues of its citizens. Yet recent studies show that the vast majority of our young people are advancing from one grade level to the next, and indeed are graduating from the public school system, with little or no knowledge of how to be an active citizen, let alone what the term "civics" really means. Therefore, students need more formal instruction about the basic principles of civic life, politics, and government, and they need it at all levels.

1. What sentence best describes the writer's purpose in the essay that will develop from this introduction?

   a. To explain what civics is and why it is no longer emphasized in the schools.

   b. To persuade people of the need to place more emphasis on civics in the public school curriculum.

   c. To describe what will happen to society if civics is no longer taught in the public schools.

2. How is the introduction organized?

   a. Problem–solution

   b. Cause–effect

   c. Process

3. What kind of definition does the writer use in sentence 2?

   a. literal

   b. stipulated

   c. expanded

4. What kind of definition does the writer use in sentences 3 and 4?

   a. literal

   b. stipulated

   c. expanded

5. Based on this introduction, what is the writer likely to want his readers to do as a result of reading the essay?

   a. Place their children in another school system that has more emphasis on civics.

   b. Teach their children civics at home to make up for the lack of emphasis on civics in the public school system.

   c. Encourage educators to change the curriculum to place more emphasis on civics.

5. Complete the following sentences (5 points)

1. A metaphor _____.

    a. is a type of comparison frequently used in scientific writing

    b. is a translated word or phrase

    c. is a word or phrase that compares two things without using *like* or *as*

2. Abstract nouns _____.

    a. refer to ideas or concepts

    b. refer to physical objects

    c. refer to dreams and fantasies

3. A literal definition _____.

    a. explains the meaning of a word within a particular context

    b. explains the meaning of a word as it is generally defined in a dictionary

    c. provides context for understanding a word

4. A stipulated definition _____.

    a. explains the meaning of a word within a particular context

    b. explains the meaning of a word as it is generally defined in a dictionary

    c. provides context for understanding a word

5. Both literal and stipulated definitions are useful in writing _____.

    a. introductions

    b. conclusions

    c. brainstorming notes

Name _____   **Date** _____

1. Match each word with its definition. (5 points)

____ 1. medication   a. stopping illness or injury in advance

____ 2. herbalism   b. someone who uses plants to heal

____ 3. preventative   c. remedy for illness or injury

____ 4. therapeutic   d. spiritual person who uses magic for cures

____ 5. diagnosis   e. a drug

____ 6. herbalist   f. something used for healing or cures

____ 7. medicine   g. the practice of healing with plants

____ 8. shaman   h. drugs in general, or a field of study

____ 9. treatment   i. determining the cause of illness/injury

____ 10. practitioner   j. person who practices a profession or technique

2. Organize the notes below into a thesis statement and complex (point-by-point) outline for a comparison essay. (5 points)

Notes:

Retirement home 1: The Orchard

Services offered:
On-site medical facilities and staff, on-site recreation and exercises classes,
daily community and social activities.

Attitudes toward elder care:
Believes in helping the elderly maintain active and meaningful lives

Retirement home 2: Windy Pines

Services offered:
Drop-in medical staff (hospital nearby), occasional bus trips to the mall, Saturday night bingo

Attitude toward elder care:
Is committed to helping families save money

Outline:
I.   Introduction. Thesis: _____

_____

II. _____

   A. _____

   B. _____

III. _____

   A. _____

   B. _____

IV. Conclusion

3. Circle the letter of the correct answer. (5 points)

1. Which sentence is correct?

   a. Neither traditional medicine or alternative healing practices have managed to find a cure for AIDS.

   b. Neither traditional medicine nor alternative healing practices have managed to find a cure for AIDS.

   c. Both traditional medicine and alternative healing practices have not managed to find a cure for AIDS.

2. Which sentence is correct?

   a. Many people strongly believe in the power of prayer alone to help cure illnesses; conversely, some people believe that prayer is a psychological aid to getting well only if it is combined with traditional treatments.

   b. Many people strongly believe in the power of prayer alone to help cure illnesses; whereas, some people believe that prayer is a psychological aid to getting well only if it is combined with traditional treatments.

   c. Many people strongly believe in the power of prayer alone to help cure illnesses; in the same way, some people believe that prayer is a psychological aid to getting well only if it is combined with traditional treatments.

3. Which sentence is correct?

   a. Even though evidence suggests that alternative healing practices such as acupuncture really work for some people. Many people remain skeptical of them.

   b. Even though evidence suggests that alternative healing practices such as acupuncture really work for some people, many people remain skeptical of them.

   c. However evidence suggests that alternative healing practices such as acupuncture really work for some people, many people remain skeptical of them.

4. Which sentence is correct?

   a. Biology is an important course for students who wish to practice medical someday; likewise, psychology is an important course because it will prepare them to better understand their patients.

   b. Biology is an important course for students who wish to practice medication someday; similarly, psychology is an important course because it will prepare them to better understand their patients.

   c. Biology is an important course for students who wish to practice medicine someday; likewise, psychology is an important course because it will prepare them to better understand their patients.

5. Here is an example of a thesis statement for an essay: "In Western culture, the connection between the body and the mind or spirit receives relatively little consideration, whereas in non-Western cultures this connection is strongly emphasized." Does this thesis statement emphasize similarity or difference?

   a. Similarity

   b. Difference

   c. It places equal emphasis on similarity and difference.

4. Read this text and then answer the following questions. (5 points)

What was once the hottest fitness craze, aerobics, is now being replaced by the newest trend in gyms and studios around the country: yoga. Yoga studios seem to be replacing aerobics studios, and gyms and health clubs seem to offer far more yoga classes than aerobics classes these days. However, the two forms of exercise, despite appearing to be very different, have more similarities than you might imagine. Aerobics has three main benefits. It is renowned for improving cardiovascular health because of the intense workout it provides and the emphasis on monitoring one's own heart rate throughout the workout. It builds strength and flexibility. Many aerobics classes involve small weights and incorporate stretching exercises into the routines. Finally, despite its frenetic pace it can actually bring peace of mind and an ability to focus. Vigorous exercise releases chemicals in the body that can produce a calming effect later; moreover, during a routine, one must focus on the often complex choreography. It is almost impossible to become distracted or let the mind wander during and aerobics class. Yoga, despite its calm and slow appearance, has very similar benefits. It too improves cardiovascular health; you may not be breathing as hard as you do in an aerobics class, but through sustained work on the breath, and through the effort of holding complex poses, the heart receives a substantial workout. Strength and flexibility are also, as with aerobics, significant benefits. Many people notice improved flexibility after only a few yoga classes, and strength is a built-in component because yoga involves holding up your own weight during complicated poses. Additionally, peace of mind and an ability to focus are lauded as important benefits of yoga. Meditation is often incorporated into yoga classes, and again, like aerobics, the necessity of focusing on new movements and muscle groups makes it difficult for the mind to wander and worry about other things. Because these two seemingly disparate forms of exercise produce such similar benefits, and have both enjoyed great popularity, perhaps we should not be so quick to replace one trend with another. Health clubs may benefit from keeping a variety of options to offer to their clientele.

1. What sentence best describes the writer's purpose?

    a. To persuade people to take up yoga.

    b. To explain why people should take up aerobics.

    c. To compare yoga and aerobics in order to investigate the current trend toward replacing aerobics with yoga.

2. What does this paragraph emphasize?

    a. Similarities

    b. Differences

    c. Similarities and differences

3. What organizational pattern does this paragraph use?

    a. Complex comparison organization

    b. Simple comparison organization

    c. Comparison and contrast organization

4. What are the points of comparison in this paragraph?

    a. Yoga and aerobics

    b.   Gyms and health clubs compared with yoga studios

    c.   Cardiovascular benefits, strength and flexibility, calmness of mind

5. Which of these sentences from the paragraph is a specific example that supports a point?

    a.   Many aerobics classes involve small weights and incorporate stretching exercises into the routines.

    b.   It is almost impossible to become distracted or let the mind wander during and aerobics class.

    c.   Aerobics has three main benefits.

5. Complete the following sentences (5 points)

1. A *suffix* is _____.

    a.   group of letters added to the beginning of a word

    b.   a group of letters in the middle of a word

    c.   a group of letters added to the end of a word

2. In a comparison essay, you can help the reader follow your ideas by_____.

    a.   expressing all of the elements of your comparison in the thesis statement

    b.   discussing both similarities and differences

    c.   including an outline to show your organization

3. Transitional expressions in a comparison essay can be used to _____.

    a.   substitute for logic and development

    b.   highlight similarities and differences between ideas

    c.   make sentences longer and more interesting to read

4. A simple organizational pattern for a comparison essay is to _____.

    a.   discuss the two subjects by alternating between several points of comparison

    b.   discuss the two subjects by alternating between them in every other sentence, constantly moving back and forth

    c.   discuss everything about the first subject, then everything about the second subject

5. A complex organizational pattern for a comparison essay is to _____.

    a.   discuss the two subjects by alternating between several points of comparison

    b.   discuss the two subjects by alternating between them in every other sentence, constantly moving back and forth

    c.   discuss everything about the first subject, then everything about the second subject

Name _____   **Date** _____

1. Match each word with its definition. (5 points)

___	1. software	a.	permanent computer fixture for data storage
___	2. integrated	b.	device to connect computers by phone lines
___	3. monitor	c.	information stored for quick, easy access
___	4. modem	d.	computer for processing web document requests
___	5. spreadsheet	e.	vcombined, unified
___	6. DSL	f.	computer equipment
___	7. database	g.	vaccounting program with rows/columns of data
___	8. hardware	h.	computer screen
___	9. server	i.	computer programs
___	10. hard drive	j.	faster system for connecting computers without requiring phone dial-up

2. Number the sentences in order. (5 points)

____ Regan concludes by warning us that although his theory is optimistic, we should not stop efforts to protest and limit violence in the media right now; we should not simply sit around and wait for change to happen.

____ Regan emphasizes the psychologists' perspective because he says it runs counter to the dominant idea of the effect of so much violence in the media; most people, says Regan, feel that we actually become desensitized to violence the more we continue to see it.

____ According to James Regan, in his article "The Death of Violence in the Media" (*The Media Buzz,* April 2001, pg. 8-10), violence in television and movies will actually begin to decrease in the near future.

____ Regan also believe that the large number of instances of shootings carried out by adolescents has also made people begin to be weary—and wary—of violence in the media, since the adolescents who committed these crimes were often inspired by violent video games and movies.

____ Regan's theory is largely based on interviews he conducted with a number of psychologists who all tended to agree on one basic principle: that our tolerance for high levels of stress and violence is limited, and that people eventually need to stabilize and nurture their emotions.

3. Circle the letter of the correct answer. (5 points)

1. Which sentence best expresses a qualified prediction?

   a. Current developments in robotics suggest that someday people who are disabled could regain mobility with the use of robotic limbs.

   b. Current developments in robotics suggest that someday people who are disabled will regain mobility with the use of robotic limbs.

c. Current developments in robotics suggest that someday people who are disabled could be regain mobility with the use of robotic limbs.

2. Which sentence best expresses a prediction with an understood condition?

a. If more homes were designed for solar energy.

b. We will conserve more energy and save more money.

c. We would conserve more energy and save more money.

3. What is the understood condition for the example in number 2?

a. If more homes are designed for solar energy.

b. If more homes were designed for solar energy.

c. We would conserve more energy and save more money.

4. Here is an example sentence from an essay: "Schools should be investing more in 'smart rooms' that are equipped with all the latest technology." Which sentence best expresses an opposing point of view?

a. Schools should be spending their money on hiring good teachers and paying them fairly.

b. Schools should be training teachers how to use all the latest technology that they are investing in.

c. Students should be transferring to schools that are equipped with all the latest technology.

5. Here is an example sentence from an essay: "In the near future, community service will become a requirement for graduation from university programs." Which sentence best expresses an opposing point of view?

a. Most universities do not currently require community service as a part of their program, although they may recommend it and offer some options for volunteer work.

b. Some ways in which people could fulfill a community service requirement could be cleaning up local parks, volunteering in a food bank or soup kitchen, and helping out at a Special Olympics event.

c. Community service will not be an option for most students, judging by the statistics that show an increase in older students returning to school; people who are struggling to work at part-time or full-time jobs and raise a family on top of going to school have no time for community service.

4. Read this text and then answer the following questions. (5 points)

In her article "Plugging In to the Future of Language Learning," Catalina Hidalgo describes how the current trend of incorporating technology into the process of learning a foreign language is going to increase significantly in the near future. She makes three predictions about technology and language learning. First of all, says Hidalgo, many publishers already have a Web page or CD-ROM component to accompany their textbooks, and we are only going to see more of that in the future. It will become common practice, she says, for teachers to assign their students homework electronically. Hidalgo adds that as computer prices decrease, and as more and more language schools and individuals acquire the appropriate technology, electronic exercises and activities could even replace paper ones altogether. A second prediction that

Hidalgo makes is that computer software for language learning will become more and more sophisticated. We already have voice recognition software that can help students to improve pronunciation, or that can allow a student to have a conversation with the computer. At the moment, says Hidalgo, this software is still in its early stages, and has many imperfections. In the near future, however, this software will improve so much that students may not even notice the difference between conversing with a computer and a native speaker of the language, and that these programs will quickly replace pronunciation cassette tapes and books. Hidalgo's third prediction is that virtual classrooms will become more and more convenient, affordable, and attractive for many students. A virtual classroom would be a class in which the teacher and students did not meet physically in a classroom, but videoconferenced via the Internet from various locations. Assignments would be e-mailed to the instructor, then corrected and returned to the students. There might be a class web page and online message boards or chat rooms. Virtual classrooms could be particularly attractive options for professionals who find it inconvenient to leave work or family to study in another country, and yet who would like the advantage of being taught by a native speaker of English.

1. What sentence best describes the writer's purpose?

    a. To persuade people to incorporate technology into their language learning experiences.

    b. To summarize another writer's predictions about technology and language learning.

    c. To compare language learning practices today with language learning in the future.

2. Whose opinions are expressed in the text?

    a. The writer's own opinions

    b. Catalina Hidalgo's opinions

    c. Both the writer's and Catalina Hidalgo's opinions.

3. Which sentence from the paragraph indicates a qualified prediction?

    a. Hidalgo adds that as computer prices decrease, and as more and more language schools and individuals acquire the appropriate technology, electronic exercises and activities could even replace paper ones altogether.

    b. It will become common practice, she says, for teachers to assign their students homework electronically.

    c. A virtual classroom would be a class in which the teacher and students did not meet physically in a classroom, but videoconferenced via the Internet from various locations.

4. Which sentence best expresses a possible alternative opinion to a point made in Catalina Hidalgo's article?

    a. Conversing with a computer is no substitute for having face-to-face conversations because a computer cannot convey gestures, facial expressions, or genuine emotions. Therefore, conversations with a computer will always have an artificial quality and will not help a student to learn language in a truly communicative fashion.

    b. Some students do not know how to type well; therefore, their progress with technological advances may be slower.

c. If technology is going to be so important in the classroom, it will be important to train teachers how to use it.

5. What would be the best thesis statement for a possible essay *about* Catalina Hidalgo's article?

a. In her article "Plugging In to the Future of Language Learning," Catalina Hidalgo predicts how technology will change the ways in which people do homework, practice speaking, and attend class.

b. Catalina Hidalgo's article "Plugging In to the Future of Language Learning," in which she predicts how technology will change the ways in which people do homework, practice speaking, and attend class, is interesting.

c. In her article "Plugging In to the Future of Language Learning," Catalina Hidalgo predicts how technology will change the ways in which people do homework, practice speaking, and attend class; however, her predictions are unrealistic and overly optimistic.

5. Complete the following sentences (5 points)

1. The advantages of considering alternative opinions about a controversial issue are_____.
   a. limiting your own opinion and perhaps trying to change it to agree with the opposition
   b. increasing your objectivity and clarifying your own opinion
   c. predicting reactions to your opinions and determining whether or not you should continue writing the essay

2. *Qualifying* predictions about the future means_____.
   a. limiting your statements because you can't know exactly what the future holds
   b. providing further evidence to support your predictions
   c. summarizing your predictions so that a reader can understand the main ideas

3. A summary is_____.
   a. as long as the original text because it reports all the information
   b. longer than the original text because it includes the writer's personal opinion and analysis
   c. shorter than the original text because it reports only the main ideas

4. The first sentence of a summary_____.
   a. always gives the writer's own opinion about the text being summarized
   b. usually gives the author and title of the text that is being summarized
   c. gives some interesting details from the text that is being summarized, in no particular order

5. Summaries are almost always written in the_____.
   a. present tense
   b. past tense
   c. future tense

Writing Placement Test Answer Keys

Part 1 Knowledge about Writing

Example: F

1. T
2. F
3. T
4. F
5. T
6. F
7. T
8. F
9. F
10. T
11. F
12. F
13. T
14. F
15. T

Part 2 Sentence Completion

Example: C

1. B
2. B
3. C
4. B
5. A
6. B
7. D
8. A
9. A
10. C
11. B
12. A
13. C
14. C
15. D

Part 3 Organization

Example: C

1. B
2. D
3. D
4. D
5. C

Part 4 Writing Test Rubric

This rubric is to be used if you request a writing sample from your students. See page 73 for prompts.

Please rank on a scale from 0 to 5. Use 0 to describe a student's writing that does NOT match the descriptor given. Use 5 to describe a student's writing that perfectly matches the descriptor given. It is very helpful if you note examples of the student writing.

Name: _____

Date: _____

Writing Areas	Rating and Examples
Content	
Sufficient detail and a variety of adjectives have been included.	
The writing is interesting.	
Sufficient information has been provided.	
The writing is well developed.	
The writing is thought provoking.	
The vocabulary used would be appropriate for an academic paper or class.	
Organization	
The writing contains a clear beginning, middle, and end.	
The sentences are organized in a logical order.	
The paragraphs are organized in a logical order.	
Cohesion and Style	
Tenses are used consistently and/or appropriately.	
Transitions are used appropriately.	
The style used is appropriate for an academic paper.	
Grammar	
All sentences are correct. There are no run-on sentences or fragments.	
All word forms, such as irregular verb forms and plurals, are correct	
Relative clauses are used correctly and positively contribute to the writing.	
Complex sentences are used correctly and positively contribute to the overall presentation.	
Form	
Capital letters are used correctly.	
Periods and commas are used correctly.	
Sentences are properly indented.	
The forms are used correctly and add to the overall presentation.	

Answer Keys for Chapter Quizzes

Chapter 1

Part 1. (5 points)

1. d
2. g
3. i
4. f
5. a
6. j
7. c
8. e
9. b
10. h

Part 2. (5 points)

__4__ On the other hand, people who are multilingual sometimes feel that although they know several languages, they may not feel one hundred percent comfortable with any of them.

__2__ One advantage, of course, is that if you can understand and speak more than one language, you can understand and talk to more people from different cultures.

__1__ There are both advantages and disadvantages to being multilingual.

__5__ They may feel as though they are "linguistic nomads," traveling from one language to another but never using one long enough to feel at home with it.

__3__ Many people feel that you can understand a culture better when you know the language.

Part 3. (5 points)

1. b
2. b
3. c
4. a
5. c

Part 4. (5 points)

1. c
2. a
3. b
4. c
5. b

Part 5. (5 points)

1. b
2. c
3. b
4. a
5. c

Chapter 2

Part 1. (5 points)

1. d
2. i
3. g
4. e
5. g
6. a
7. h
8. j
9. c
10. b

Part 2. (5 points)

__5__ In sum, these three examples suggest that having a superior education or specialized academic background is not necessarily the most important thing.

__3__ Courage is also important, for explorers can suddenly find themselves in relative isolation and in extremely difficult or dangerous situations.

___1___ Explorers tend to exhibit three main qualities: a spirit of adventure, courage, and self-discipline.

___4___ Another important quality is self-discipline, since explorers must fight the inevitable urge to quit when things become overwhelming or difficult.

___2___ One important quality is the desire to venture across new frontiers – to go where no one has gone before in terms of distance or knowledge.

Part 3. (5 points)

1. a
2. b
3. c
4. a
5. c

Part 4. (5 points)

1. b
2. c
3. a
4. c
5. b

Part 5. (5 points)

1. b
2. c
3. b
4. a
5. c

Chapter 3

Part 1. (5 points)

1. f
2. g
3. b
4. i
5. j
6. a
7. d
8. c
9. h
10. e

Part 2. (5 points)

___4___ Women, on the other hand, tend to cross their legs, fold their hands in their lap, and sit or stand far from the person with whom they are speaking.

___2___ Another term for the "body language" that researchers have observed is nonverbal communication; it is the way in which people communicate through gestures and facial expressions.

___5___ The next time you observe men and women speaking, look for these examples of body language that have been described and ask yourself: do men's actions speak louder than women's?

___3___ Some of the researchers have found that men tend to take up more physical space, sit with their legs slightly apart, and lean in toward the person with whom they are speaking.

___1___ Some researchers, following the saying "actions speak louder than words," have observed the body language of men and women as they speak.

Part 3. (5 points)

1. a
2. c
3. b
4. c
5. c

Part 4. (5 points)

1. a
2. c
3. c
4. b
5. b

Part 5. (5 points)

1. b
2. c
3. c
4. a
5. b

Chapter 4

Part 1. (5 points)

1. i
2. f
3. g
4. h
5. c
6. a
7. j
8. d
9. b
10. e

Part 2. (5 points)

3   Then you can see how the lines resemble animals and geometric shapes.

5   They wonder how and why the ancient Nazca culture made these incredible pictures.

1   The giant Nazca lines in Peru are too big to be seen in their entirety from the ground.

4   Many people have speculated about them.

2   Therefore, it is necessary to view them from an airplane.

Part 3. (5 points)

1. c
2. a
3. c
4. c
5. b

Part 4. (5 points)

1. b
2. b
3. a
4. c
5. c

Part 5. (5 points)

1. b
2. b
3. a
4. c
5. c

Chapter 5

Part 1. (5 points)

1. f
2. d
3. a
4. g
5. i
6. h
7. b
8. j
9. e
10. c

Part 2. (5 points)

3   The ceremony typically occurs when the child turns thirteen.

2   The names of these ceremonies indicate whether they are for boys or for girls; Bar Mitvah means "Son of the Commandments" and Bat Mitvah means "Daughter of the Commandments."

1   In the Jewish religious tradition, the Bar and Bat Mitvah ceremonies celebrate a boy or a girl's becoming an adult.

5   Later, he or she celebrates with friends and family at a big party.

4   First the child reads from the Torah (the Five Books of Moses).

Part 3. (5 points)

1. c
2. a
3. b
4. b
5. c

Part 4. (5 points)

1. c
2. a
3. b
4. c
5. b

Part 5. (5 points)

1. b
2. a
3. b
4. c
5. c

Chapter 6

Part 1. (5 points)

1. e
2. f
3. j
4. g
5. b
6. c
7. d
8. a
9. h
10. i

Part 2. (5 points)

1 Dreams
  2 Psychological interpretations
    3 Freud's theory of the unconscious
      4 A recurring dream about a house might symbolize your personal health.
  2 Physiological aspects
    3 The brain stem sends signals to the cortex, which turns signals into dream stories
      4 People you see randomly in the day may be stored as memory and transmitted to you in your dreams later.

Part 3. (5 points)

1. b
2. c
3. a
4. c
5. a

Part 4. (5 points)

1. a
2. b
3. c
4. b
5. b

Part 5. (5 points)

1. c
2. b
3. a
4. b
5. a

Chapter 7

Part 1. (5 points)

1. f
2. h
3. g
4. c
5. j
6. d
7. i
8. a
9. e
10. b

Part 2. (5 points)

I. a – f : Thesis Statement: Studying a foreign language for many years in school can lead to increased job opportunities later on.

II. a – b – c : (a) Studying a foreign language for many years in school can lead to (b) increased proficiency in the language, which in turn can lead to (c) increased interest in the culture / place in which the language is spoken.

III. d – e – f : (d) Increased interest in the culture can lead to a desire or opportunity to travel there, which results in (e) total immersion in the culture and proficiency in the language, which ultimately can result in (f) job opportunities, either in that culture or elsewhere.

Part 3. (5 points)

1. b
2. c
3. b
4. a
5. c

Part 4. (5 points)

1. a
2. b
3. a
4. c
5. c

Part 5. (5 points)

1. c
2. b
3. b
4. c
5. b

Chapter 8

Part 1. (5 points)

1. f
2. i
3. e
4. a
5. c
6. j
7. d
8. b
9. g
10. h

Part 2. (5 points)

__4__ Other questions to ask yourself would be: do I want to study in an urban, suburban, or rural environment? How long are the classes? What resources are available?

__5__ Finally, you will probably need two or three letters of recommendation from people who know you or your work well; be sure to request these letters far enough in advance so that your references can compose thoughtful, accurate letters.

__3__ Your next step should be to select the schools that most fit your interests and request application materials.

__2__ To begin, you should think about your goals and conduct careful research about schools and their courses of study.

__1__ There are several preliminary steps to follow in order to apply for a university program and maximize your chances of being accepted into the program of your choice.

Part 3. (5 points)

1. b
2. c
3. a
4. b
5. c

Part 4. (5 points)

1. b
2. a
3. c
4. b
5. a

Part 5. (5 points)

1. c
2. b
3. b
4. a
5. c

Chapter 9

Part 1. (5 points)

1. f
2. i
3. e
4. b
5. h
6. c
7. j
8. d
9. a
10. g

Part 2. (5 points)

___4___ Folk art can also come in many different forms, including paintings, drawings, sculpture, furniture, needlework, and pottery, to name just a few.

___5___ Despite confusion over the term and its examples, a growing number of folk art museums and folk art gallery exhibits suggest that there is increasing interest in the genre and that we ought to take it more seriously.

___1___ *Folk art* is a term that is often misapplied or misunderstood, perhaps because it can come in so many different forms.

___3___ The term *folk art* can also be used to describe craft techniques that have been passed down through generations, or to describe art produced by an untrained artisan that reflects a region, a culture, or a religious tradition.

___1___ Before explaining the various forms it can come in, we should first establish the fact that the basic definition of *folk art* is that it is art produced by a self-trained artist – that is, an artist who has received no formal training and is an "outsider" to the elite art community.

Part 3. (5 points)

1. b
2. a
3. b
4. c
5. a

Part 4. (5 points)

1. b
2. b
3. c
4. a
5. c

Part 5. (5 points)

1. b
2. c
3. a
4. b
5. a

Chapter 10

Part 1. (5 points)

1. c
2. j
3. f
4. i
5. b
6. a
7. h
8. d
9. e
10. g

Part 2. (5 points)

___2___ We anticipate many problems resulting from the development of this new branch of the national Big Values chain.

___1___ We the undersigned are writing in protest of the proposed new Big Values store that is scheduled to open in Pleasant Town in May of 2002.

    4   There is an additional concern about the proximity of the planned Big Values store to a children's playground; the constant traffic that would result from the megastore could pose safety hazards to the children, not to mention destroy the face of our town common.

    3   The biggest problem we foresee is that it will cause the failure of most of many stores in Pleasant Town which are small, family-run businesses that cannot hope to compete with Big Values.

    5   There is an undeveloped area of land off of a major highway that could be accessed by several towns, including Pleasant Town, without defacing any of them or directly harming their business. Perhaps this is a solution that you could consider.

Part 3. (5 points)

1. c
2. a
3. b
4. b
5. a

Part 4. (5 points)

1. b
2. a
3. a
4. b
5. c

Part 5. (5 points)

1. c
2. a
3. b
4. a
5. a

Chapter 11

Part 1. (5 points)

1. e
2. g
3. a
4. f
5. i
6. b
7. h
8. d
9. c
10. j

Part 2. (5 points)

I. Introduction. Thesis: Two retirement homes, The Orchard and Windy Pines, are quite different in terms of the services they offer and their attitudes toward elder care.

II. Services offered:
    A. The Orchard—on-site medical facilities and staff, on-site recreation and exercise classes, daily community social activities
    B. Windy Pines—drop-in medical staff (hospital nearby), occasional bus trips to the mall, Saturday night bingo

III. Attitudes toward elder care:
    A. The Orchard—believes in helping the elderly maintain active and meaningful lives
    B. Windy Pines—is committed to helping families save money

IV. Conclusion

Part 3. (5 points)

1. b
2. a
3. b
4. c
5. b

Part 4. (5 points)

1. c
2. a
3. b
4. c
5. a

Part 5. (5 points)

1. c
2. a
3. b
4. c
5. a

Chapter 12

Part 1. (5 points)

1. i
2. e
3. h
4. b
5. g
6. j
7. c
8. f
9. d
10. a

Part 2. (5 points)

__5__   Regan concludes by warning us that although his theory is optimistic, we should not stop efforts to protest and limit violence in the media right now; we should not simply sit around and wait for change to happen.

__3__   Regan emphasizes the psychologists' perspective because he says it runs counter to the dominant idea of the effect of so much violence in the media; most people, says Regan, feel that we actually become desensitized to violence the more we continue to see it.

__1__   According to James Regan, in his article "The Death of Violence in the Media" (*The Media Buzz*, April 2001, pg. 8-10), violence in television and movies will actually begin to decrease in the near future.

__4__   Regan also believe that the large number of instances of shootings carried out by adolescents has also made people begin to be weary—and wary—of violence in the media, since the adolescents who committed these crimes were often inspired by violent video games and movies.

__2__   Regan's theory is largely based on interviews he conducted with a number of psychologists who all tended to agree on one basic principle: that our tolerance for high levels of stress and violence is limited, and that people eventually need to stabilize and nurture their emotions.

Part 3. (5 points)

1. a
2. c
3. b
4. a
5. c

Part 4. (5 points)

1. b
2. b
3. a
4. a
5. c

Part 5. (5 points)

1. b
2. a
3. c
4. b
5. a